About this book

Symbols are used to denote the following categories:

➕ map reference to maps on cover

✉ address or location

☎ telephone number

🕐 opening times

✋ admission charge

🍴 restaurant or café on premises or nearby

Ⓜ nearest underground train station

🚌 nearest bus/tram route

🚃 nearest overground train station

⛴ nearest ferry stop

✈ nearest airport

❓ other practical information

ℹ tourist information office

➤ indicates the page where you will find a fuller description

This book is divided into five sections.

The essence of Barbados pages 6–19
Introduction; Features; Food and drink; Short break

Planning pages 20–33
Before you go; Getting there; Getting around; Being there

Best places to see pages 34–55
The unmissable highlights of any visit to Barbados

Best things to do pages 56–77
Great cafés; stunning views; places to take the children and more

Exploring pages 78–153
The best places to visit in Barbados, organized by area

💎 to 💎💎💎💎💎 denotes AAA rating

Maps

All map references are to the maps on the covers. For example, Bathsheba has the reference ➕ 4F – indicating the grid square in which it is to be found

Admission prices

Inexpensive (under Bds$15); moderate (Bds$15–35); expensive (over Bds$35)

Hotel prices

Prices are per room per night: $ budget (under US$100); $$ moderate (US$100–350); $$$ expensive to luxury (over US$350). Where possible the author has adjusted the rating of all-inclusive hotels to reflect the true quality of the hotel.

Restaurant prices

Price for a three-course meal per person without drinks: $ budget (under Bds$60); $$ moderate (Bds$60–110); $$$ expensive (over Bds$110)

Contents

THE ESSENCE OF...

6 – 19

PLANNING

20 – 33

BEST PLACES TO SEE

34 – 55

ESSENTIAL
BARBADOS

★ Best places to see 34–55

Northern Barbados 99–130

◼ Featured sight

Bridgetown and Around 80–98

Southern Barbados 131–153

Original text by Lee Karen Stow
Revised and updated by Polly Roger Brown

© AA Media Limited 2010
First published 2008. Revised 2010

ISBN: 978-0-7495-6670-8

Published by AA Publishing, a trading name of AA Media Limited, whose registered
office is Fanum House, Basing View, Basingstoke, Hampshire RG21 4EA.
Registered number 06112600.

AA Media Limited retains the copyright in the original edition © 2001 and in all
subsequent editions, reprints and amendments

A CIP catalogue record for this book is available from the British Library

n a retrieval
ying,
ias been
wise
t in which it
is publication
ccept no
he
t your
ised upon the
ect the
racy, but
ections.

Colour separation: MRM Graphics Ltd
Printed and bound in Italy by Printer Trento S.r.l.

A04192
Maps in this title produced from:
  map data supplied by Global Mapping, Brackley, UK © 2010
  map data © Borch GmbH
  map data from Mountain High Maps ® Copyright © 1993 Digital Wisdom, Inc

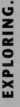

BEST THINGS TO DO

EXPLORING...

56 – 77

78 – 153

The essence of...

Introduction   8–9

Features   10–11

Food and drink   12–15

Short break   16–19

THE ESSENCE OF BARBADOS

Silvery beaches, the warm, translucent, turquoise sea and some of the Caribbean's finest hotels make Barbados one of the world's most desirable holiday destinations. But this is also an island with soul, where gospel singing and the Friday night fish fry are as important as the international polo matches and the annual opera season; a place where cricket is not just a passion, but a national obsession.

Barbados may be less scenically dramatic than some of its volcanic, rainforested neighbors but it is welcoming, safe and rich in colonial history; the perfect place for a relaxing and unforgettable vacation.

features

Barbados enjoys a high repeat-visitor factor, but it's not just sun, sea and sand that attracts tourists. Barbadians are known to be among the friendliest people in the Caribbean and visitors who have found the soul of Barbados and forged friendships are those that have been coming back to the island for 20 years or more.

Barbados has gained a reputation as a celebrity hotspot. An eclectic mix of politicians, movie stars, supermodels and musicians all holiday in luxurious private villas and exclusive resorts along the West Coast.

Meanwhile, Barbados and its population of 284,000 carries on as it has done since tourism succeeded the sugar cane industry. Locals and visitors alike enjoy the island's mix of attractions: from natural formations of limestone caves and hidden gullies; beautiful beaches lapped softly by ripples from the Caribbean Sea or swept by the crashing surf of the

Atlantic; to its glittering crop of restaurants and food shacks serving Barbadian (Bajan) food and locally produced rum and beer.

Despite more than 40 years of independence from Great Britain, a quaint Englishness still exists, with cricket on the green, afternoon tea and horse racing. Enriching these traditions are African arts, crafts and songs – roots unearthed by Barbadians whose ancestors were brought here centuries ago as slaves to work the sugar plantations.

In 2007 the Cricket World Cup put the island in the spotlight when the final was held in the now state-of-the-art Kensington oval. Many of the existing attractions were given a facelift for the big event and the thousands of additional visitors it brought. This is an ongoing process and Barbados has several excellent new museums as well as two attractive wooden boardwalks which run along stretches of the seafront on the South and West Coasts, allowing people to stroll by the ocean in comfort and safety.

food & drink

Barbadian fare is built on dishes of African origin, spiced up for the Caribbean with English-inspired, cucumber sandwiches thrown in for good measure.

NATIONAL DISHES

The premier national dish is flying fish, a silvery-blue, sardine-like fish that actually thrashes its tail to enable it to glide above the surface of the sea. Once de-boned, the fish is rolled in breadcrumbs and Bajan seasoning, then deep fried. Other catches of the day are barracuda, dolphin (or dorado, sometimes listed on the menu as *mahi mahi* and a fish, not a dolphin), tuna, kingfish and snapper. Lobster and shrimp harvested in Guyana are grilled and drizzled with oil or smothered in sauces.

Fish is blended into a chowder or battered as fishcakes and served with the island's own hot pepper sauce. Take care with the ubiquitous bottle of

Bajan sauce placed on the table. One dash is enough, three is explosive. For real local food, seek out a cook shop and watch all parts of a chicken, pig or black-bellied sheep go in a pot for simmering. Pudding and souse is actually a sausage made from sweet potato (pudding) served with boiled pig's head and feet (souse) and a cucumber and pepper pickle.

Another national dish is *cou-cou*, made from cornmeal similar to the African dish *foo-foo*. Primarily, the local diet is rich in starch, derived from sweet potatoes, yams and fried plantains (like a banana but cooked before eating). Breadfruit was introduced to the island by Captain Bligh of *Mutiny on the Bounty* fame, and pumpkins are made into a delicious soup. Rice mixed with peas is a popular side dish, as is macaroni cheese pie. Look for set-priced Bajan buffets where you help yourself to a

dozen typical dishes. For fast food, Bajans prefer chicken, or a roti filled with meat or fish curry. For dessert, try mango, passion fruit, cherries, papaya, or coconut sweet pie and butter pudding.

ALCOHOLIC DRINKS

A rum shop is a small bar and local haunt where Bajans discuss cricket and politics and play dominoes or the old African game called *warri*. They order a plate of fish and a shot of rum, which comes dark or as clear as pure vodka. The connoisseur usually selects a five-year-old blend. Drink it neat, with crushed ice, with cola, or shaken into a cocktail. Hotels and bars concoct their own mindblowers. Daiquiri is a delicious blend of mango

or banana pulp, rum, lime juice, ice and sugar. Gin and coconut water also goes down well. Banks beer is for

sale everywhere and is best drunk ice-cold from the bottle.

NON-ALCOHOLIC DRINKS

English afternoon tea served complete with a tier of cakes, cream scones and cucumber sandwiches is a tradition in many hotels on the west coast. For sheer refreshment choose from chilled ginger beer or a fresh coconut, its top hacked off and a straw plunged into the milk. *Sorrel* is a Christmas drink, made from plant leaves infused in hot water and spices. Bars sell fruit punches and real juices, lemonade actually made from lemons and internationally known brands of cola and canned drinks.

TASTY SNACKS

There are plenty of snack to keep you munching on Barbados. Try tamarind balls, coconut turnovers and jam puffs. In November *conkies*, sweet potato pudding made with raisins and served in banana leaves, are sold all over. *Cutters* are small sandwiches, the best of which are filled with flying fish.

short break

If you only have a short time to visit Barbados, or would like to get a really complete picture of the country, here are the essentials:

● **Spend a day in Bridgetown** (➤ 81) shopping for tax-free jewelry, clothes and handicrafts, then stroll along the riverside boardwalk.

● **Snorkel on the west coast and look for wild turtles,** or go diving to see them glide through the water (➤ 67).

● **Take a picnic to Bathsheba** (➤ 40) on the east coast and watch the waves crash onto the cliffs and beaches.

● **Listen to gospel singing** and enjoy Sunday brunch at The Crane beach hotel (➤ 146), overlooking the dramatic Atlantic coast.

● **Eat fried flying fish and macaroni cheese pie** or rice at the famous Oistins Fish Market (➤ 149) on Friday and Saturday nights.

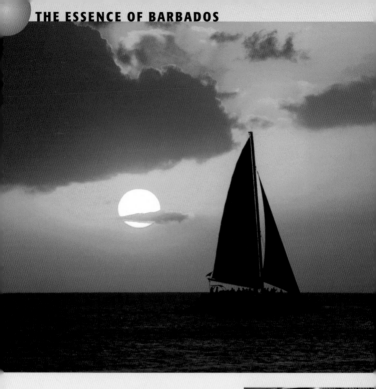

- **Take a sunset cruise,** or forget your cares on one of many party cruises that leave Bridgetown every day (➤ 62).

- **Visit a rum factory to learn how the national drink is made,** then sample it and purchase a bottle to take home (➤ 135).

- **Ride on an electric tram** through the limestone formations of Harrison's Cave (➤ 48), the island's famous attraction renovated in 2009.

● **Dive to a depth of 147ft (45m) on the Atlantis Submarine** (➤ 144) to see a shipwreck, stingrays, turtles and shoals of colorful tropical fish – without getting wet.

● **Stroll through the terraces of plants** at the Andromeda Botanic Gardens (➤ 36), the extraordinary legacy of one woman.

Planning

Before you go   22–24

Getting there   25

Getting around   26–28

Being there   29–33

Before you go

WHEN TO GO

JAN	FEB	MAR	APR	MAY	JUN	JUL	AUG	SEP	OCT	NOV	DEC
27°C	27°C	27°C	27°C	27°C	27°C	31°C	31°C	27°C	27°C	27°C	27°C
81°F	81°F	81°F	81°F	81°F	81°F	88°F	88°F	81°F	81°F	81°F	81°F

🟦 High season 🟦 Low season

Barbados enjoys a tropical climate with an average daytime high of 75–85°F (24–29°C) and slightly cooler nights. The rainy season is from June to November, with short, sharp showers most afternoons, followed by warm sunshine again. If hurricanes are going to develop, they usually do so between June and October, but Barbados tends to be outside their path as the island is a long way east and separate from the main Caribbean chain of land masses. The last direct hit was in 1955.

WHAT YOU NEED

		UK	Germany	USA	Netherlands	Spain
●	Required					
○	Suggested					
▲	Not required					

Some countries require a passport to remain valid for a minimum period (usually at least six months) beyond the date of entry – contact their consulate or embassy or your travel agency for details.

	UK	Germany	USA	Netherlands	Spain
Passport valid for 6 months beyond date of departure/national ID card	●	●	●	●	●
Visa (regulations can change – check before booking your trip)	▲	▲	▲	▲	▲
Onward or return ticket	●	●	●	●	▲
Health inoculations (polio, tetanus, typhoid, hepatitis A)	○	○	○	○	○
Health documentation (➤ 23, Health Insurance)	○	○	○	○	○
Travel insurance	○	○	○	○	○
Driving license (national or international)	●	●	●	●	●
Car insurance certificate (if own car)	○	○	○	○	○
Car registration document (if own car)	▲	▲	▲	▲	▲

WEBSITES

The official site of the Barbados Tourist Authority is www.visitbarbados.org

Other useful websites include www.barbados.org and www.funbarbados.com

TOURIST OFFICES AT HOME

In the UK

Barbados Tourism Authority
263 Tottenham Court Road
London
W1T 7LA
☎ 020 7636 9448

In the USA

Barbados Tourism Authority
820 Second Avenue
Fifth Floor
New York
NY 10017
☎ 212 551 4350
Toll Free 1 800 221 9831

HEALTH INSURANCE

If you fall ill, hotels can arrange a doctor to come and see you. If things get serious, the hospital is never far away on this small island. Full medical insurance is highly recommended and should cover you for medical and hospital costs, transportation to a suitable off-island medical facility if required, repatriation and permanent disability. Note that you will need additional coverage for certain sports such as scuba diving.

TIME DIFFERENCES

GMT	Barbados	Germany	USA (NY)	Netherlands	Spain
12 noon	8AM	1PM	7AM	1PM	1PM

Barbados is four hours behind the UK, five hours in British Summer Time. The island is one hour ahead of East Coast Time. Time does, however, take on different meaning in the Caribbean and visitors should expect to slow their pace accordingly.

NATIONAL HOLIDAYS

January 1 *New Year's Day*
January 22 *Errol Barrow Day*
March or April *Easter*
April 28 *National Heroes Day*

May 1 *Labor Day*
Last Monday in May *Whit Monday*
August 1 *Emancipation Day*
August 6 *Kadooment Day*

November 30 *Independence Day*
December 25 *Christmas Day*
December 26 *Boxing Day*

WHAT'S ON WHEN

December–May Polo season, with fixtures at the island's four fields.

January *Barbados Jazz Festival.* One week of live jazz from top musicians. At Sunbury Plantation House and Farley Hill.

February *Holetown Festival.* A week-long celebration of the first settlement of the island; fashion shows, sporting events and parades.

February/March *Sandy Lane Gold Cup Garrison Savannah.* The year's most glamorous and prestigious horse race.

March *Holders Season.* Two weeks of music, opera and theater at Holders House, St James. A society event attracting people from all over the world.

April *Fish Festival.* A celebration of the fruits of the sea, with dancing, music and a lot of fish at Oistins.

May *Gospelfest*, attracting singers and choirs from all over the Caribbean. *Bridgetown Film Festival.*

July/August *Crop Over.* The year's biggest event, traditionally celebrating a successful sugar cane harvest. Five weeks of parades, live bands, calypso music and exhibitions, culminating in the lavish Grand Kadooment carnival parade.

November *National Independence Festival of Creative Arts* Concerts. Plays and exhibitions culminating with a parade. *Independence Pro Surfing Championships.* Prestigious competition held at Bathsheba's Soup Bowl.

Getting there

BY AIR

Grantley Adams International Airport

9 miles (15km) to city center

🚋 N/A

🚌 40 minutes

🚗 30 minutes

Barbados is served by, among others, American Airlines, Air Jamaica, US Airways, Air Canada, British Airways, Virgin Atlantic and LIAT. Visitors arrive at Grantley Adams International Airport in the south. It is the island's only airport and has been extensively refurbished. Now, there are shops, exchange facilities and restaurants. British Airways and BWIA offer first- and business-class lounges. Departing passengers pay a tax of US$27.50 or Bds$55, though this is almost always included in air fares.
Airport and flight information ☎ 418 4242; www.gaiainc.bb.

BY SEA

Cruise passengers dock at the harbor in Bridgetown, at the stylish Cruise Passenger Terminal, with duty-free (tax-free) shopping, banking and other facilities.

Getting around

PUBLIC TRANSPORTATION

Internal flights There are no internal flights within Barbados. LIAT, Caribbean Airlines, Air Jamaica, SVG Air and Trans Island Air operate flights to neighboring islands in the Caribbean.

Trains There are no rail services on Barbados.

Buses Buses are an excellent, inexpensive way of getting around. Frequent services run to most parts of the island and all services terminate in Speightstown. A flat fare of Bds$1.50 takes you anywhere. There are two main types of bus: government-owned (blue with a yellow stripe ☎ 310 3500) for which you must have the correct fare, and privately owned mini buses (yellow with a blue stripe) which give change. Destinations are clearly marked on the front or painted on the sides. From Bridgetown, buses run from terminals on Fairchild Street for the south and from Lower Green to the west coast and north. In addition to the main buses there are also the privately owned ZRs, these mini buses, which are white with a maroon stripe, leave from Probyn Street, River Road and Cheapside terminals.

Boat trips Boats are another good option of public transportation. Several organized tours of the coastline are available, plus trips to neighboring Caribbean islands.

EXCURSIONS

Numerous companies offer tours of the island; some of them, like Island Safari (➤ 153), in four-wheel drive vehicles, take visitors off-road through the sugar-cane fields and along the east coast to beautiful and remote beach spots (➤ 60–61). The Barbados Transport Board runs scenic tours of the island every Sunday. Buses leave Independence Square in Bridgetown at 2pm and make several stops along the way. Each Sunday in the month buses ply a different route. Fares are Bds$15. For further information ☎ 228 6023. If you book a tour, many of the tour companies will pick you up from your hotel.

WALKING

The Barbados National Trust organizes regular hikes for three levels of ability, in the morning, afternoon or moonlight. This is a great way to see the island and meet local people. The hikes are free, although donations are welcome. For a calendar, visit www.trust.funbarbados.com.

FARES AND TICKETS

If your're booking through a tour operator ask about the Barbados VIP Card, valid from April to December (excluding the Crop Over festival period in July) and offering "buy one, get one free" deals at most main attractions. The Barbados Gourmet Card gives members 25 percent off the bill in selected restaurants, valid from April to December. Some attractions have two levels of pricing, one for locals and one for visitors; this reflects the lower incomes that local Bajans receive, and that the government encourages locals to make the most of their island.

TAXIS

Cabs may be expensive but they can make sense if there are a number of you who want to travel around. Identified by ZR number plates or painted white with a taxi sign on the roof, the cabs are clean, efficient and many have air conditioning. There are no meters, but fares are regulated by the government and published by the tourist office in Bridgetown. Expect to pay around Bds$40 from the airport to the south coast, or Bds$90 from the airport to Speightstown. Taxis can be hired for private tours, too, at about US$35 per hour. This is often worthwhile as the drivers are very knowledgeable and are full of gossip and local lore.

DRIVING

- Speed limit on highways: 50mph/80kph
- Speed limit on main roads: 30mph/50kph (inner city 25mph/40kph)
- Speed limit on minor roads: 30mph/50kph (inner city 25mph/40kph)
- Seat belts must be worn at all times and in rear seats where fitted.
- Although there are no specific limits on drinking and driving, you should always drive with due care and attention. You may find that your insurance cover is not valid for accidents if you drink and drive.
- Fuel is available in leaded, unleaded, premium and diesel. Bridgetown has one 24-hour fuel station. Others around the island have varying opening and closing times. Most close on Sundays, so you are advised to fill up before you travel at weekends.
- In the event of a breakdown contact your rental agency, which will either send help or replace the vehicle.

CAR RENTAL

Choose anything from a Mini Moke to an air-conditioned sedan. Rent on arrival at the airport or from your hotel. Vehicles can be hired for an hour, day, week or longer on production of a current driving license and a major credit card. You must buy a driving permit for Bds$10, issued from the car rental companies or the Ministry of Transport ☎ 429 2191. To rent a car, you must be over 21 and under 75. Bicycles and mopeds are also available for rent.

Being there

TOURIST OFFICES
The head office of the Barbados Tourism Authority
(☎ 427 2623) is on Harbour Road, Bridgetown and
there are booths at the airport and the cruise terminal.

MONEY
Barbados's currency is the Barbados dollar (Bds$) which is fixed against
the US dollar (Bds$2=US$1) and divided into 100 cents. Both US and
Barbados dollars are accepted, and major credit cards can be used at
most hotels, restaurants and stores. International banks include Barclays
Bank plc and Canadian Imperial Bank of Commerce. At Grantley Adams
International Airport, the Barbados Bank is open daily from 8am until the
last flight departs.

TIPS/GRATUITIES

Yes ✓   No ✗

Restaurants (10–15% service usually included)	✗	
Cafés/bars (10% service included)	✗	
Tour guides	✓	US$10
Taxis	✓	10% of the fare
Chambermaids	✓	US$2.50 a room per day
Cloakroom attendants	✓	US$2.50
Toilets	✓	change
Porters	✓	US$1 per bag

POSTAL AND INTERNET SERVICES
The main post office is in Cheapside, Bridgetown ☎ 436 4800 🕐 Mon–Fri
8–5. Each parish has its own smaller post office 🕐 usually 8–3. Mail boxes
are red. Most hotels and resorts have internet facilities and many have WiFi
throughout (usually free of charge). Every shopping mall on the island has
at least one internet café – though hourly rates are not cheap
(Bds$20/US$10 per hour). The chain of Italia coffee houses (Holetown,
Bridgetown and the south coast) has free WiFi for customers.

TELEPHONES

Satellite links and direct dialing are available. All local calls are free except from pay phones, where 25 cent coins are needed. Barbados has 95 percent coverage from the Digicel cellular network as well as cable and wireless. Phones set up for GSM 900, 1800 or 1900 will work on the island. Check roaming costs with your provider at home before traveling.

International dialing codes

From Barbados to:
UK 0 11 44
Germany 0 11 49
USA and Canada 0 11 1
Netherlands 00 11 31

Emergency telephone numbers

Police 211
Fire 311
Ambulance 511

EMBASSIES AND CONSULATES

UK ✉ British High Commission, Lower Collymore Rock, Bridgetown
☎ 430 7851
Germany ✉ Brittons Hill, St Michael
☎ 427 1876
Netherlands ✉ Norton Lilly Barbados Ltd, 2nd Floor Atlantis Building, The Shallow Draught, Bridgetown
☎ 436 1101
USA ✉ Wildey Business Park, Wildey, St Michael ☎ 227 4000

HEALTH ADVICE

Sun advice The Caribbean sun is extremely strong and you must protect your skin. Choose a good-quality, high sun protection factor sunscreen and reapply frequently, especially after swimming and water sports. Avoid the midday sun. Wear good sunglasses and, if possible, a wide-brimmed hat. Limit your time in the sun when first going to the beach. If you do suffer

sunburn, stay out of the sun until you recover. Beach vendors sell aloe vera, which is very soothing for sunburn. If headache, nausea or dizziness occur, call a doctor.

Drugs Prescriptions and non-prescription drugs and medicines are available from pharmacies.

Safe water Barbados water is very pure, having been filtered by the island's natural coral. It can be enjoyed straight from the tap.

PERSONAL SAFETY

You may be approached and asked to buy marijuana or harder drugs. Politely refuse and walk away. Keep a close eye on belongings and, if possible, leave valuables in the hotel safe or room safe. Don't walk the beaches at night and avoid unfamiliar neighborhoods. Don't leave valuables in cars.

ELECTRICITY

The power supply in Barbados is 110 volts 50 cycles. Carry an adapter to make sure your appliances fit the two-prong sockets. Many hotels can also supply adapters.

OPENING HOURS

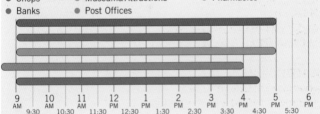

Some stores also open on Saturday mornings 9–1. Museums open slightly later in high season. Banks open 9–5 on Fridays. Pharmacies also open on Saturdays 8–1. Some open 24 hours but not all. Pharmacies include Grants in Oistins ☎ 428 9481; Jems in Holetown ☎ 432 6997; and Knights on Lower Broad Street, Bridgetown ☎ 426 5196; and most shopping malls on the island have a pharmacy.

LANGUAGE

As a result of 300 years of British rule, the official language of Barbados is English and all islanders speak and understand it fluently. However, among themselves, Barbadians speak a dialect, known simply as Bajan, which has been heavily influenced by the African languages brought to the island by slaves, and sounds very different to English. Spoken with an almost impenetrable accent, it is a distinctive and highly expressive form of speech, particularly rich in wise sayings. Most bookshops on the island sell books on How to Speak Bajan for those who are interested. Here are some of the best-loved Bajan proverbs:

Evah pig got 'e Saturday	*Everyone has a day of retribution*
Eggs have no right at rockstone dance	*Don't get into situations you can't deal with*
Trouble don't set up like rain	*Bad times are unpredictable*
Every bush is a man	*There are always people eavesdropping, wherever you are*
Mek sure better than cock sure	*Better to make certain than make assumptions*
If greedy wait, hot will cool	*All things come to he who waits*
The sea en' got no back yard	*There are some scrapes you might not get out of*

And here are some Bajan words that you will hear frequently:

Bim	*Barbados*
Cheese-on-bread	*You don't say!*
Dingolay	*Dance*
In a short-short	*Very soon*
Juk	*Poke/stab*
Liming	*Hanging out*
Nyam	*Eat (a lot)*
Malicious	*Nosy*
Snap	*Shot (of rum)*
Wuh loss	*Wow! What!*
Wunna	*You (plural)*

Best places to see

Andromeda Botanic Gardens   36–37

Barbados Wildlife Reserve   38–39

Bathsheba   40–41

Chalky Mount Potteries   42–43

Flower Forest and Orchid World   44–45

Garrison Historic Area   46–47

Harrison's Cave   48–49

National Heroes Square, Bridgetown 50–51

Speightstown   52–53

Sunbury Plantation House   54–55

1 Andromeda Botanic Gardens

A profusion of both indigenous and tropical plants and flowers pays tribute to the mythical Greek princess Andromeda in this garden by the ocean.

Bathsheba (➤ 40), on the rugged eastern coastline, makes a dramatic setting for this garden, established in 1954 by the late amateur horticulturist Mrs Iris Bannochie. Mrs Bannochie devoted herself to the garden, creating trails of blossoms and tropical foliage on the cliffs above the Atlantic, and collected many rare species of plant on her trips around the world. She named her creation after Andromeda (daughter of King Cepheus of Ethiopia) who, according to legend, was chained at the water's edge as a sacrifice to the sea monster before being rescued by Perseus.

Cascading streams and waterfalls have been added, and the gardens are building up a collection of medicinal plants with information on their traditional uses. Andromeda is astonishingly beautiful, awash with frangipani *(Plumeria rubra)*, bougainvillaea *(Bougainvillaea spectabilis)*, traveler's trees *(Ravenala madagascariensis)* and orchids *(Orchidaceae)*. Through strategically scattered palms you

glimpse the azure blue of the ocean from viewpoints on the pathways. The fishing village in the distance is Tent Bay. As you admire Andromeda, Barbados monkeys swing in the trees above, and there are mongooses and lizards.

In 1988, before her death, Iris Bannochie donated her gardens to the Barbados National Trust. The Trust now offers tours led by Andromeda's own gardeners on Wednesdays at 10:30am. If you prefer to go it alone, there's a choice of two self-guided trails, one covering hilly areas and taking up to an hour, and the other a half-hour, easier stroll.

🚩 4F ✉ Bathsheba, St Joseph ☎ 433 9261 or 433 9384 ⏰ Daily 9–5 (except public holidays) 🏛 Moderate, children half price 🍴 Light meals, snacks and afternoon tea served at the Hibiscus Café ($$). The cook will also prepare a picnic lunch for you to eat in the gardens 🚌 From Bridgetown, Speightstown ❓ Further information from the Barbados National Trust (☎ 433 9384, http://trust.funbarbados.com)

2 Barbados Wildlife Reserve

This natural mahogany forest is probably most known as home to a collection of exotic animals, birds and reptiles, but it also features buildings made of coral stone and relics left over from the island's sugar industry.

While sipping a cold drink at the mahogany bar here, don't be surprised to see a red-footed Barbados tortoise stroll by. Except for caged parrots and a python, the animals here mostly roam freely over the 4 acres (1.5ha) of forest. The reserve is built from coral stone gathered from surrounding canefields and its paths are made of bricks (still carrying the manufacturer's stamp) from 17th- and 18th-century sugar factories.

Children love it here, but they must be supervised as some of the animals, including the monkeys, can bite. Among the mix are cattle egrets, spectacled caimans, guinea fowl, deer, pelicans, congas, flamingos, cockatoos, toucans and peacocks. In a straw-carpeted pen, iguanas of the West Indies, the largest vertebrates native to the Caribbean islands, sprawl on logs. They bake in the sun, oblivious to the rabbits hopping

around them and the juvenile tortoises crawling by. Many creatures arrived here as gifts to the reserve. The agoutis and the armadillos are from the forestry departments in St Lucia and St Vincent, while the pelicans hail from Florida.

To see the Barbados green (or vervet) monkeys, be here between 2 and 3pm, when the colony returns from the forests of nearby Grenade Hall (▶ 112). Originally introduced from West Africa, the monkeys number around 5,000–7,000 on the island and just one animal can provide up to 2.5 million doses of polio vaccine. The reserve's Primate Research Center, focusing on the use and conservation of the monkey, is responsible for up to 70 percent of the world's production of the vaccine.

✚ 2E 🖂 Farley Hill, St Peter ☎ 422 8826 🕓 Daily 10–5 (last admission 3:45) ✋ Moderate, children half price. Includes admission to Grenade Hall Forest and Signal Station 🍴 Café ($) 🚌 Regular bus service from Bridgetown, Holetown, Speightstown and Bathsheba ❓ Several sightseeing operators visit the reserve

3 Bathsheba

This tiny beauty spot on the east coast has a great appeal for those wanting to see the rugged, natural face of Barbados.

There are no luxury hotels at Bathsheba and you won't find anyone to park your car. Even in peak season, this fishing village is devoid of crowds. Its coves and bays are washed by excellent surf and surfing champions ride the waves from September to December at the frothy Soup Bowl at the center of the beach. Two rows of giant, grass-covered boulders seem to guard the bay from the threat of the approaching tide. In fact, apart from the bathing pools that fill up and can be enjoyed at low tide, it's far too dangerous to swim here.

What you can do, though, is stroll by the church and the pastel-painted houses or wander along the deserted beaches backed by chalky cliffs and wild hills. There are no formal attractions here, just the peace and scenery. Nearby are the green hills of Cattlewash, so-called because the cattle wander down to the ocean to take a bath.

In Victorian times, Bathsheba was a magnet for vacationing

Barbadians who would come to take the air. A railroad once ran from Bridgetown to Bathsheba but closed in 1937. Its life was precarious, suffering from landslides and underfunding. Coastal erosion was so bad the crew often had to get out to repair the track. Today the old railway line is a scenic walking route, though going the whole distance from Bathsheba to Bridgetown takes a full day.

Bathsheba is due to get its first luxury boutique hotel, built on the site of the original Atlantis Hotel in nearby Tent Bay.

✚ 4F 🍴 New Edgewater Hotel ($) – for the Sunday Bajan buffet, 12–3, book in advance (▶ 125) 🚌 Regular bus service from Bridgetown, Holetown and Speightstown

4 Chalky Mount Potteries

You can watch pottery being made and fired traditionally and enjoy fabulous views of the Scotland District in the chalk hills of St Andrew.

The highly skilled potter Winston Junior Paul and his wife, Prim, run Highland Pottery, a uniquely placed workshop high in Chalky Mount Village. It stands on a geological formation said to resemble a sleeping man with his hands folded over his stomach. Locals refer to it as "Napoleon." At one time over 20 pottery businesses thrived here, the studios and workshops humming in wood houses high on the hills. Today, only a couple struggle to make a living, battling against cheap imports. Beneath them is the brown-red clay dug to create the artists' pieces. Winston's workshop is like a tree house, open on all sides to let in the refreshing breezes. It has a fine

360-degree view of the undulating eastern landscape, known as the Scotland District, that rambles down to the Atlantic.

Winston tells you how the clay is first mixed with water then sieved to take out the tree roots. The mixture is then laid out on drying trays in the sun for about three weeks until the water has evaporated. Next it is brought indoors, where the rushing wind dries out the last of the water. He invites you to watch him knead the clay on the wedging table, squeezing out the bubbles before slapping it down on the potter's wheel. Before the advent of electricity, pots were thrown on a kick wheel, which is made of cement and shaped like a millstone. The wheel is kicked to rotate the clay and Winston is so skilled at it that he appears to be running while shaping a flower vase before your eyes. He then fires the pots in the kiln, after which they are painted and glazed and displayed on shelves.

🔧 3F ✉ Chalky Mount Potteries, Chalky Mount, Scotland District ☎ 422 9818 🕐 Daily 9–5 💷 Free 🍴 Restaurants/cafés ($–$$) at Bathsheba 🚌 From Bridgetown

5 Flower Forest and Orchid World

This colorful duo, featuring tropical and native trees and spectacular orchids, lies on a popular scenic route in the parishes of St Joseph and St John.

Flower Forest

Set 846ft (258m) above sea level on a former sugar plantation, the 50-acre (20ha) forest has a visitor center that is furnished with old copper sugar-boiling vats and decorated with a mural depicting the plantation's history. From here a nature trail leads through a tropical corridor of neatly labeled plants and trees. Look for the native bearded fig tree *(Ficus citrifolia)*, bamboos and breadfruit *(Artocarpus altilis)*, plus the Queen of Flowers tree. Some rest spots overlook beautifully manicured lawns, the most splendid being Liv's Lookout, with views of the rugged Scotland District and the island's highest point, Mount Hillaby, at 1,115ft (340m).

Orchid World

Opened by the then Prime Minister Owen Arthur, Orchid World lies in the high-rainfall area of the island, which averages 79in (203cm) annually. Rainwater is collected in a 29,920-gal (136,000 liter) tank and, as much as possible, recycled. This

makes for a healthy environment for a plethora of orchid species that is continually being added to. Orchids spring up everywhere, and *vandas*, *schomburgkia* and *oncidium* grow by the paths. *Epiphytes*, or air plants, dangle from wire frames in the specially controlled environment of the orchid houses. Coral, limestone rockeries, caves and a babbling stream add to the tranquillity of the garden, which has a far-reaching view across the silvery sheen of the sugar-cane fields.

Flower Forest
✚ 3F ✉ Richmond, St Joseph ☎ 433 8152 ⏱ Daily 9–5
(last tour 4pm) 💰 Moderate 🍴 On-site café ($) 🚌 From
Bridgetown take the Chalky Mount or Sugar Hill bus and ask
the driver to drop you off near the forest

Orchid World
✚ 3H ✉ Between Gun Hill and St John's Church,
Highway 3b ☎ 433 0306 ⏱ Daily 9–5 (last admission 4:30)
💰 Moderate 🍴 Café ($) 🚌 From Bridgetown take the
Sargeant Street bus

6 Garrison Historic Area

Once the defense nucleus of Barbados, the Garrison consists of a circle of mid-17th-century military buildings and an exceptional cannon collection.

When Oliver Cromwell took control of England after the Civil War of 1648, he set his sights on Barbados. But Lord Willoughby, the governor of Barbados, decided to strengthen the island's defense. Needham's Fort, later renamed Charles Fort, today stands as the oldest building, dating back to 1650. It was strengthened by the addition of another fort, St Ann's, now the headquarters of the Barbados Defense Force.

When France declared war on Britain in 1778, an influx of British troops arrived at the Garrison. The bewildered Barbados government, which had trouble finding enough accommodations for them, was forced to build temporary barracks. The majority of troops left when the war ended. A permanent garrison building was built to accommodate the soldiers who stayed and to prevent future attacks on the British islands. Over the years the Garrison has seen many alterations but the distinctive redbrick clock tower of

the Main Guard has changed little. The 30 or so 17th- to 18th-century cannons, from perhaps the world's largest collection, are housed within the Barbados Defense Force Compound at St Ann's Fort.

Since the withdrawal of the British troops from Barbados in 1905–1906, some buildings have been refurbished. The latest to receive attention is Bush Hill House, where the United States' first president, George Washington, stayed in 1751. The house is now known as George Washington House and is open to the public (▶ 143).

Horse racing takes place on the Garrison Savannah, the former parade ground. By day cricket teams practice their batting and fielding, while locals jog around the track. It was here, on November 20, 1966, that the British Union Flag was lowered and Barbados's blue and gold flag – bearing a trident – raised to mark Independence Day.

✚ 2K ✉ St Michael ✋ Free 🍴 Brown Sugar ($$–$$$)
(▶ 58) 🚌 From Bridgetown and the south coast ❓ 1.5-hour tours of the Garrison area. Own transportation needed
☎ 228 2925

7 Harrison's Cave

www.harrisonscave.com

A ride on an electric tram takes you through the subterranean stream passages of a natural limestone wonder – the island's most famous site.

A labyrinth of creamy white stalagmites and stalactites dripping with rainwater, Harrison's Cave is a world away from the tropical jungle above it. Deep below the island's geographical center, you don a hard hat and hop aboard a trolley car for a 1-mile (1.5km) long guided tour. Following a smooth underground passageway, you halt to photograph the "cathedral" chamber, a waterfall pouring into an 8ft (2.5m) deep pool. Nearby is a group of conical shapes known as "people's village." Alongside runs the original subterranean stream. Above hangs the "chandelier," continuously dripping with calcite-laden water. The stalactites and stalagmites have been growing over thousands of years and in some places have joined together to form pillars.

Although named after Thomas Harris, who owned most of the land in the area during the early 1700s, the caves were actually discovered in 1796

by Dr George Pinckard, an English doctor who lived on the island. Several expeditions were attempted during the 18th and 19th centuries but with little success and it was not until the 1970s that the true extent of this natural wonder was revealed by a Danish speleologist and Barbadian cavers. Government-backed explorations and excavations followed and an underground stream was diverted as work on creating an attraction began.

The first tourists arrived in 1981 and the cave has since welcomed Queen Elizabeth II and musicians Paul McCartney and Elton John. The full story of the caves and how they were discovered is explained in an audiovisual show in a special theater, shown before the tour gets underway.

The cave is one of the island's "must see" sights. The site reopened in February 2010 following major refurbishment and now has a new restaurant, Interpretation Center and a number of green initiatives.

✚ 3G ✉ Welchman Hall, St Thomas
☎ 438 6640 ⏱ Tours daily at half-hourly intervals. First tour 9am, last tour 4
💲 Expensive 🍴 Snack bar ($–$$) on site
🚌 Bus from Bridgetown signposted Shorey Village

8 National Heroes Square, Bridgetown

Originally planned to represent London's Trafalgar Square in miniature, the capital's focal point is becoming increasingly Barbadian.

Before April 28, 1999, this main square was known as Trafalgar Square, a throwback to the days when Barbados was known as Little England. The square was renamed by the Prime Minister, Owen Arthur, in a ceremony that took place to mark the occasion of the second National Heroes Day. It is a holiday

that remembers notable figures in the island's history. Taxi drivers and locals, however, still call it Trafalgar Square.

During the ceremony, 10 people were honored, including Errol Walton Barrow, the first prime minister elected after independence in 1966; Bussa, the slave leader of the 1816 rebellion; cricket star Sir Garfield Sobers; and Samuel Jackman Prescod. Prescod, the son of a slave mother, rose in 1843 to become the country's first non-white member of Parliament in more than 200 years. He fought for the rights of all classes and colors.

A bronze statue of Lord Nelson was erected in the square in 1813. Nelson sailed to the island in 1805 with a large fleet, which included the *Victory*, months before he perished at the Battle of Trafalgar. For decades there has been talk of moving Nelson (he's considered a defender of the slave trade) elsewhere and erecting a Barbadian figure, possibly that of Barrow, instead.

Opposite the admiral towers the obelisk honoring the Barbadians killed in World Wars I and II. In the center, the Dolphin Fountain commemorates the first running water piped to the town. Surrounding the square are the neo-Gothic buildings of the seat of Parliament, including the Treasury and House of Assembly and the new Museum of Parliament and National Heroes Gallery (➤ 85). This is an ideal starting point for a walking tour of the capital.

➕ *Bridgetown 5d* ✉ Junction of Broad Street and St Michael's Row, Bridgetown, St Michael 👆 Free 🍴 Numerous cafés and restaurants ($–$$) on Broad Street and along the Careenage 🚌 All buses run to Bridgetown

9 Speightstown

Brightly colored fishing boats, wooden houses and a quaint church make up this typical West Indian settlement, Barbados's second-biggest town.

Speightstown (pronounced "Spitestown") might appear sleepy, but the calm is broken when the fishing boats come in and locals arrive in their hoards to shop. It bears a history as a thriving port for sugar and the old commercial part is gradually being restored by the Barbados National Trust. Arlington House, one of the National Trust's properties, has been beautifully restored and is open to the public as an Interpretive Center with an emphasis on local history.

The town offers modern shopping in the Mall, bakeries serving Bajan bread, and market stalls of fruit and vegetables. There's also the chance to while away the hours in a rum shop with the Bajans on a Saturday afternoon, listening to cricket on the radio.

Founded by William Speight, Speightstown was the principal export destination for the island's sugar. Because of the town's importance, military forts were built around it for protection but today little remains of this defensive ring.

St Peter's Parish Church, one of the earliest churches on the island, dates from around 1630. Inside, the wooden gallery above was once occupied by the "poor whites," the name given to descendants of English, Irish and Scots who were imported as indentured labor to work on the sugarcane plantations.

A "Round de Town" stroll and the longer, more challenging award-winning Arbib Nature and Heritage Trail (➤ 122) organized by the Barbados National Trust both begin by the painted blue benches at the harborside, just past the Fisherman's pub.

🚦 1E ✉ Speightstown, St Peter 🚌 Buses from all over the island ❓ A 2-hour "Round de Town" stroll runs on Wed, Thu and Sat (or by alternative arrangement) from 9:30am or 2:30pm, depending on numbers (☎ 426 2421 🅿 Moderate)

10 Sunbury Plantation House

www.barbadosgreathouse.com

Bordered by gardens, this 340-year-old plantation house is crammed to the ceiling with relics from the days of the great white sugar planters.

For the best insight into how the wealthy white planters lorded it up while their slaves and laborers sweated, step inside Sunbury Plantation House. You're immediately surrounded by trappings of the rich, an outstanding collection of Victorian and Edwardian pottery, silverware and china. Anywhere else such a trove would be roped off or protected behind glass show cabinets. At Sunbury, where all the rooms are accessible, you walk among the Barbados mahogany tables and antiques as though you're waiting for the owner to return.

Originally thought to be called Chapmans, after one of the first planter families, Sunbury is now owned by Mr and Mrs Keith Melville. The house was opened to the public in 1983. Highlights include the sunroom, furnished with a white rattan suite, where the ladies would mingle. Men conducted business in the office, the only room to contain the house's original curios, including a 1905 calculator. Portraits of wealthy landowners hang alongside drawings of scenes from the West Indies during the days of slavery. Upstairs, the airy bedrooms are a treat. Check out the 1920s swimming costume, the marble hip bath and the lady's silver brush set on the dressing table.

🔢 4J 📧 St Philip ☎ 423 6270 🕓 Daily 10–5 💰 Moderate 🍴 Courtyard restaurant and bar ($–$$) 🚌 From Oistins to College Savannah or Bayfield ❓ A planter's candlelit dinner at Sunbury includes a five-course meal, cocktails, all drinks and a tour of the house. Reservations required. Minimum number of 10

Best things to do

Good places to have lunch   58–59

Best beaches   60–61

Places to take the children   62–63

A walk to Mullins Bay   64–65

Top places for diving   66–67

Stunning views   68–69

A drive along the ABC Highway   70–71

Top activities   72–73

Best places to stay   74–75

Best cultural activities   76–77

Good places to have lunch

▽▽▽ Al Fresco ($$)

The elegant restaurant at the Treasure Beach Hotel opens out onto the property's pretty hideaway garden. There's a daily three-course lunch menu that offers light Caribbean cuisine at reasonable rates.

✉ Paynes Bay, Holetown ☎ 432 1346; www.treasurebeachhotel.com

▽▽ Brown Sugar ($$–$$$)

Beautiful setting on a fern-filled patio with cool splashing water. Creole fish chowder, pepper chicken and coconut-beer shrimp are specialties. The lunchtime Bajan Buffet is excellent value.

✉ St Michael ☎ 426 7684; www.brownsugarbarbados.com

▽▽▽ Cobblers Cove ($$$)

The Terrace restaurant within this elegant hotel is right on the waterfront and the lunchtime menu is light and delicious. Gourmet salads and wraps feature daily as well as fish caught each morning by the hotel's own fisherman.

✉ Cobblers Cove, St Peter ☎ 422 2291; www.cobblerscove.com

Hibiscus Café ($)

Light meals, Bajan snacks and delicious rum punch in a pretty little café in lovely gardens. The cook will prepare a picnic if you'd like to eat among the exotic blooms or on the lawns (► 36–37).

✉ Andromeda Botanic Gardens ☎ 433 9384

▽▽▽ Mullins ($$–$$$)

An attractive and informal restaurant set right on one of Barbados's loveliest beaches. Listen to turquoise waves lap the sand while you choose from an extensive menu that includes sandwiches, wraps and rotis, as well as pasta dishes, pizza and burgers.

✉ Mullins Bay, St Peter ☎ 422 2044; www.mullinsbarbados.com

Patisserie Flindt ($$)

Escape the midday sun on an elegant and classy shaded terrace in the center of Holetown. The home-made cakes are fabulous and there are lots of other dishes on offer, such as imaginative salads, fancy sandwiches and thin-crust pizza.

✉ Holetown, St James ☎ 432 2626; www.flindtbarbados.com

Best beaches

Barbados has around 69 miles (112km) of coastline and public beaches. The west is calm enough for swimming, snorkeling and water-skiing; the south is for windsurfing; and the east is the domain of experienced surfers and bodyboarders.

Accra Beach
This south coast beach is usually packed with well-toned people sunbathing, strutting around or bodysurfing; great for posing.
✚ 2K

Bathsheba
Pounded by the Atlantic Ocean and scattered with strange boulders. Bathsheba's coast is breathtaking though the current makes it too dangerous for swimming (➤ 40).
✚ 4F

Bottom Bay
This bay is one of the most beautiful spots on the island. Admire the views then head down the cliff steps and weave through the palms that decorate the white sands.
✚ 6H

Crane Bay

This east coast bay is beloved for its high cliffs plunging down to pink-tinged sands and a white-tipped ocean, perfect for surfing.

✚ 6J

Fitts Village

Fitts Village offers good snorkeling and is within reach of the Malibu Beach Club, which has its own beach, offering water sports and volleyball. A visitor center shows you how Malibu rum is made.

✚ 1H

Mullins Bay

A busy, west-coast favorite where you can do anything, from snorkeling to jet skiing. Sit in a deckchair and have your hair beaded, sunbathe, or enjoy a cocktail at the bar. Gibbes Bay, to the south, is quieter.

✚ 1F

Paynes Bay

Paynes Bay has palm trees growing out of the sand and hawkers selling assorted goods and sun loungers.

✚ 1G

Sandy Beach

This beach is ideal for families as it is protected by a reef that creates a calm, shallow lagoon. It's also a great place to learn windsurfing.

✚ 2K

Silver Sands

On the southern tip of the island, this beach is home to windsurfing experts, though intermediate windsurfers can take lessons (➤ 141).

✚ 4L

Places to take the children

Aerial Trek

Older children will love this adrenaline-fueled attraction in the middle of the island. Eight zip-lines snake high above a deep gully and amusing guides ensure that everyone whizzes from one platform to the next safely while relating interesting facts about the age-old flora and fauna (➤ 100).

✉ Jack-in-the-box Gully, Walkes Spring Plantation, St Thomas ☎ 438 8735; www.aerialtrek.com

Atlantis Submarine

A real submarine taking day and night dives to the bottom of the ocean, with views of coral gardens, wrecks and tropical fish (➤ 144). If you are lucky you might see a turtle swimming by. Children are awarded a certificate after the dive.

✉ Shallow Draught, Bridgetown ☎ 436 8968; www.atlantisadventures.com

Barbados Wildlife Reserve

Watch tortoises roam freely around the reserve and rabbits hop around the iguanas in the pen. Barbados green monkeys are often seen swinging through the trees around 2–3pm when food is laid out for them (➤ 38).

✉ Farley Hill, St Peter ☎ 422 8826 🕐 Daily 10–5 (last admission 3:45)

Harbour Master Cruises

A lunchtime cruise along the coast on a huge, four-deck vessel with onboard craft demonstrations, Bajan food and, best of all, a 70ft (21m) water slide.

☎ 430 0900; www.tallshipscruises.com

Harrison's Cave

Stalactites, stalagmites and an electric tram ride underground that children will love. Reopened in 2010 after a huge refurbishment, this is one of the island's best attractions (➤ 48).

✉ Welchman Hall, St Thomas ☎ 438 6640; www.harrisonscave.com

a walk to Mullins Bay

This is an easy-going stroll along the beach punctuated by swimming and sunning, and ending with a fantastic sunset. The walk is mainly on the beach but there are some stretches of road involved.

From Speightstown (▶ 52), follow the lane leading to the beach and turn left into the curve of a cove, overlooked by the Cobblers Cove hotel (▶ 74).

Here early evening strollers may have witnessed the mass exodus of turtle hatchlings, heading from their nests to the ocean. If you come across baby turtles, don't handle them

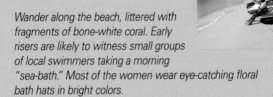

as they will become disoriented and may never find the water.

Wander along the beach, littered with fragments of bone-white coral. Early risers are likely to witness small groups of local swimmers taking a morning "sea-bath." Most of the women wear eye-catching floral bath hats in bright colors.

Notice the occasional coconut palms bending almost horizontally to the water. On Barbados everything from this tree is used. The fruit makes a coconut drink, the flesh is scraped and used in baking scones (biscuits), the husk for souvenirs, the trunk for building houses and the palm fronds for weaving baskets.

Pass wooden beach shacks where women sit outside and scrape the scales off fish. You may see the square fishing baskets that are left on the seabed for days until the fish swim in and become trapped. Often there is a fisherman at the shoreline casting out his fishing net.

Rounding the corner you'll see the full stretch of Mullins Bay and its neat rows of sunloungers. Here there are several water-sports operators and a small shack selling beachwear. This is a good place to sit at the beach bar and drink a pina colada before retracing your steps back along the beach. Or you could return along the coastal road, or take the bus.

Distance 0.6 miles (1km)
Time Half to a full day with swimming and stops
Start Point Speightstown beach ✚ 1E
End Point Mullins Bay ✚ 1F
Lunch Mullins ($$) (▶ 58) ✉ Mullins Bay ☎ 422 2044

Top places for diving

There are two main areas on the island for diving – the calm
Caribbean west coast and the waters around Carlisle Bay in
Bridgetown. Favorite dive sites include several spectacular
wrecked ships and a number of offshore reefs.

Dottins
Part of the Folkstone Marine Park in Holetown, the reef is teeming
with schools of iridescent fish and beautifully colored coral. ✚ 1G

Maycocks
Running east to west rather than parallel to the coast, Maycocks
has particularly spectacular fish life, with parrotfish, barracuda,
large rays and amazing sponge formations. ✚ 1D

Palmir

On the northern end of the west coast, this average-sized shipwreck in shallow waters is perfect for beginners. ✛ 1E

Spawnee

A shallow reef that gives inexperienced divers the opportunity to see fish more commonly associated with deeper sites, like Caribbean reef squid and Trumpet fish. ✛ 1F

SS Stavronikita

Regarded as the ultimate wreck dive, this freighter has a wealth of cabins and corridors to explore. ✛ 1H

Dive schools cater for all abilities. The following are all members of the Professional Association of Dive Operators Barbados (PADO):

Barbados Blue

✉ The Hilton, Carlisle Bay, St Michael
☎ 435 5764; www.divebarbadosblue.com

High Tide Dive Shop

✉ Coral Reef Club, St James
☎ 432 0931; www.divehightide.com

Reefers and Wreckers

✉ Timothy House, Speightstown
☎ 422 5450; www.scubadiving.bb

West Side Scuba Centre

✉ Baku Beach, Holetown
☎ 439 2558; www.westsidescuba.com

Stunning views

- Bathsheba (➤ 40)

- Cherry Tree Hill (➤ 119)

- Cove Bay

- Gun Hill (➤ 134)

- Hackleton's Cliff

- Mullins Bay (➤ 61, 64–65)

- North Point (➤ 119)

- Ragged Point (➤ 137)

- Royal Westmoreland Golf Course

- Silver Sands (➤ 61, 141)

a drive along the ABC Highway

A drive along the modern Adams Barrow Cummins Highway (ABC) is a journey through Barbados's history. Many commuters head in and out of Bridgetown daily, so avoid morning and evening traffic. At lunchtime the traffic situation is better, and Sundays are ideal. The highway links the Grantley Adams International Airport with the west coast road, the Ronald Mapp Highway, up to Speightstown. It is named after three of the island's statesmen: Tom Adams (prime minister from 1976 to 1985); Errol Barrow (prime minister from 1966 to 1976 and 1986 to 1987); and Gordon Cummins (premier from 1958 to 1961).

Start at the roundabout near the University of the West Indies and take the ABC marked route, heading east.

Traditional scenery of cane fields and chattel houses contrasts with sleek buildings, car showrooms, banks and the island's television station. On a Sunday the Highway is lined with coconut sellers – the water inside a green coconut makes a refreshing and nutritious drink. At the top of the St Barnabas Highway is the Freed Slave, also known as Bussa or the Emancipation Statue. A heroic figure in the island's history, Bussa was blamed for leading the slave rebellion of 1816 in which many were killed, executed or deported. So long as you park safely and take care crossing the roundabout, you can reach the steps up to the statue base to take a photo.

Back at the roundabout, you can take a detour west along Two Mile Hill toward Government House, once the home of John Pilgrim, a Quaker. The governor of Barbados lives there now. Get back on the ABC Highway and head south along St Barnabas Highway to the Garfield Sobers Roundabout. At the next roundabout (Errol Barrow) go straight on to St Lawrence Gap (▶ 140), a hive of souvenir shops, bars and cafés.

Park and explore the Gap or just head down to the expanses of sand at Rockley or Dover beaches.

Distance 5 miles (8km)
Time 2 hours
Start Point Roundabout near University of the West Indies ✚ 1J
End Point St Lawrence Gap ✚ 2K
Lunch Excellent choice in St Lawrence Gap ($–$$$) (▶ 147–150)

Top activities

● Watch a game of cricket, the national passion of Barbados, at the Kensington Oval in Bridgetown (➤ 98).

● Bet on the horses at the historic Garrison Savannah (➤ 47). Turf Club of Barbados at the Garrison (☎ 426 3980; www.barbadosturfclub.com) will be waiting to take your bets.

● At Sea Spray Water Sports, Holetown (☎ 249 5001; www.seaspraywatersports.com), snorkel with the turtles – but don't feed them.

● Go on a four-wheel drive adventure safari with Island Safari (➤ 153), the perfect way to get an insider's view of Barbados.

● Take a Sunday stroll with the Barbados National Trust (➤ 27) and learn about local mythology and history.

● Hop aboard their catamaran and let Silver Moon Catamaran sailing cruises (➤ 98) make you feel like a millionaire for a day.

● Try your swing at the Sandy Lane Country Club golf course (➤ 130), which offers basic pay-and-play and stunning views.

● Go horseback riding at the Highland Adventure Centre (Cane Field, St Thomas ☎ 438 8069).

● Let Surf Barbados (➤ 153) teach you to bodyboard in the gentle rollers off the south coast.

● Drop a line and catch a large fish like marlin, tuna or shark; I.O.U. Charters (☎ 429 1050; www.ioucchartersbarbados.net) will be happy to oblige.

Best places to stay

▽▽▽ Almond Beach Village ($$–$$$)

Large all-inclusive property divided into several areas, for couples, families, luxury and so on. Numerous pools and a beautiful beach. Superb childcare and many dining options (➤ 124).

▽▽▽ Cobblers Cove ($$$)

Country house-style hotel on the west coast with beautiful colonial decor, wonderful food and an English feel. The Terrace restaurant is one of the most romantic on the island (➤ 58, 124).

▽▽▽ Coral Reef Club ($$)

Stay in coral stone cottages surrounding a pretty, plantation-style house. The hotel has been owned by the same family for five decades and the service, as a result, is impeccable (➤ 124).

⬧⬧ Discovery Bay by Rex Resorts ($$)

Popular all-inclusive in a charming old plantation-style property at the northern end of Speightstown. Secluded gardens, beach and a large pool on site (➤ 124).

⬧⬧ ⬧⬧ Fairmont Royal Pavilion Hotel ($$$)

Luxury resort hotel set in beautiful, lush gardens on the west coast (➤ 125).

⬧⬧⬧ Lone Star Restaurant and Hotel ($$–$$$)

Just four simple but luxurious suites and the new Beach House, which attracts an A-list clientele, belonging to the legendary Lone Star bar and restaurant (➤ 127).

⬧⬧⬧ The Sandpiper ($$)

Boutique hotel in Holetown, set in tropical gardens and fronting a sandy beach. Sister hotel of the Coral Reef Club, with which it shares facilities (➤ 125).

⬧⬧ ⬧⬧ Sandy Lane ($$$)

The *grande dame* of Barbados hotels. Lavish in every way, with a spectacular spa, impressive children's club, enormous lagoon pool and exclusive dining (➤ 126).

⬧⬧⬧ Sea Breeze Resort ($$)

All-inclusive hotel with a lovely stretch of beach and excellent dining options (➤ 146).

⬧⬧⬧ Treasure Beach ($$)

Intimate, popular hotel with 35 suites in traditional Caribbean architectural style, set in a horseshoe shape around the pretty pool. The deluxe suites have private plunge pools (➤ 126).

Best cultural activities

● Attend a National Cultural Foundation event that includes a wide range of visual and performing arts shows. The NCF (✉ West Terrace, St James ☎ 424 0909; www.ncf.bb) also organizes the popular National Independence Festival of Creative Arts (NIFCA) every November, which is a key part of Barbadian independence celebrations.

● Be dazzled by verbal dexterity at a reading given by the poets and novelists of Voices, the Barbados Writers Collective (www.voicesbarbadoswriterscollective.cariblogger.com).

● Browse through the fascinating collection of books on Barbados in the small resource center at the Springvale Eco-Heritage Museum, Springvale Plantation (➤ 120).

● Go to a live classical, contemporary or jazz concert at the prestigious Frank Collymore Hall in Bridgetown (✉ Central Bank of Barbados, Spry Street, Bridgetown ☎ 436 9083; www.fch.org.bb).

● Listen to an expert lecture on the island's history, characters and culture at the Barbados Museum (➤ 91).

● Mingle with arts students from all over the Caribbean and witness their efforts in dance, drama and musical performance at the Errol Barrow Centre for Creative Imagination, part of the University of the West Indies (✉ UWI, Cave Hill Campus, Cave Hill, St Michael ☎ 417 4776; www.cavehill.uwi.edu).

● Tune in to the Voice of Barbados, a local radio station with a mix of excellent and informative daily phone-in shows, soap operas in Bajan dialect and vivid debates on matters political and social (VOB 92.7; www.vob92.9.com).

● Visit a privately owned house as part of the Barbados National Trust's Open House program (☎ 426 2421; www.nationaltrustbarbados.com). A dozen homes on the island open their doors every Wednesday afternoon between January and March each year – these include swanky villas at Sandy Lane, the Prime Minister's home and restored 18th-century plantation houses.

● Watch an outdoors movie at the Globe Drive-In (✉ Adam's Castle, Christ Church ☎ 437 0479) or catch the monthly moonlit screenings of vintage films on the seafront at the Star Bar in Speightstown (☎ 234 2494).

Exploring

Bridgetown and Around   81–98

Northern Barbados   99–130

Southern Barbados   131–153

Settled by Arawak Indians, who harvested the rich fishing grounds, the north is the least developed part of the island today. Millions of blades of sugar cane, silvery in the sunlight, bend toward the white surf. Similarly unspoiled is the east coast, with the hilly Scotland District plunging down to sand and palm beaches.

The south and west are the tourist hubs, each very different in character – and price. Bridgetown is the busiest place on the island; particularly so when the big cruise ships arrive in port, mainly in the winter months. In contrast, rising up to the highlands in the center of the island are patches of tropical forest above limestone caves.

It's possible to drive around the island in one day, but you'd be wiser exploring sections at a time and taking a long lunch, out of the midday heat. Alternatively, round up some friends for a swim: a beach is never far away.

Bridgetown and Around

Bridgetown □

The town was originally known as Indian River Bridge, after the discovery of an Amerindian bridge spanning the Constitution River here. Founded by British settlers in 1628, it grew up to become the island's administrative and commercial capital and principal port. Before independence in 1966 Bridgetown bowed under British sovereignty, which is why there are traces of English character in its colonial architecture. With the sumptuously furnished houses of the sugar planters and

warehouses stocked with goods from around the globe, Bridgetown was compared to wealthy Port Royal in Jamaica before the latter was wiped out by an earthquake.

The bulk of Barbados's 284,000 population lives in and around the capital, with an estimated 100,000 actually within the city and suburbs. The capital is the seat of the Barbados government, with the British monarch holding executive powers and represented on the island by a governor general, who in turn advises the cabinet and appoints the prime minister. Next come 21 members of the Senate and a 28-member House of Assembly, residing in the Parliament Buildings.

Most of the attractions can be seen in half a day on a walking tour starting near National Heroes Square (also known as Trafalgar Square (► 51), with the rest of the day spent shopping and trying out the cafés and restaurants. Bridgetown is also a base for day cruises, yacht charters, or a trip on the Atlantis Submarine (► 144) and a day's cricket at the Kensington Oval (► 98).

BRIDGETOWN SYNAGOGUE

Tucked away off Magazine Lane and worth a visit is the Jewish Synagogue. Next door is a Jewish cemetery where weathered tombs contain the remains of Jews who arrived in Bridgetown in the 17th century and set up businesses on nearby Swan Street. The synagogue dates back to 1654, but was rebuilt in the 19th century following extensive hurricane damage. Remarkably well kept by the Barbados National Trust, it is believed to be one of the oldest synagogues in the western hemisphere. Inside, gorgeous wood paneling is brightened by the light from a quartet of brass chandeliers. Members of the island's present Jewish population still use the synagogue on a regular basis.

🔷 *Bridgetown 4c* ✉ Synagogue Lane, off Magazine Lane ☎ Barbados National Trust, 426 2421 🕐 Mon–Fri 9–12, 1–4 ✋ Free, donations welcome 🚌 Fairchild Street

THE CAREENAGE

Alongside the Careenage – a narrow inner harbor at the mouth of the Constitution River – a wooden boardwalk accented with ornate, green-painted street lamps takes you past dozens of charter yachts and ocean-going boats advertising tours and deep-sea fishing. On the other side of the harbor are the many restored and painted houses of The Wharf. Toward the town, the boardwalk leads back to the main square or across Chamberlain Bridge to Independence Arch. Built in 1987, this monument commemorates the 21st anniversary of the island's independence.

✚ *Bridgetown 3e* ✉ The Wharf, off National Heroes Square 🖐 Free 🍴 Waterfront cafés ($–$$) 🚌 Fairchild Street, main bus terminal

MONTEFIORE FOUNTAIN

The Montefiore Fountain, built in memory of a Jewish businessman called John Montefiore, was originally installed in Beckwith Place. Its position today, on what looks like a traffic island in Coleridge Street, seems inappropriate for such a beauty. Look closely and you'll see the figures of Fortitude, Temperance, Patience and Justice portrayed. The accompanying inscription reads, "Look to the end; Be sober-minded; To bear is to conquer; Do wrong to no one."

✚ *Bridgetown 4b* ✉ Coleridge Street
✋ Free 🚌 Fairchild Street

NATIONAL HEROES SQUARE

Best places to see ➤ 50–51.

PARLIAMENT BUILDINGS

Though Barbados has the third-oldest parliament in the whole of the Commonwealth, established in 1639 with an all-white House of Assembly, the Parliament Buildings to the north of National Heroes Square are younger. This is due to the number of fires that blighted the town, the most devastating occurring in 1766. Following the fire of 1860, the Parliament Buildings you see now were built in neo-Gothic style. This group includes the Senate and the House of Assembly, the latter fitted with stained-glass windows depicting British monarchs and Oliver Cromwell. The clock tower is not the original; that was demolished in 1884 and a new one built two years later in 1886. Here sat the decision-makers, colonists of the 1700s busily reaping the rewards of sugar-cane farming. You can imagine them fretting over whether the "mother country," England, would interfere with their right to self-government, or whether their slaves were plotting to rebel. The West Wing has been refurbished and now houses the **Museum of Parliament and the National Heroes Gallery**, a small but well-planned interactive display that details the history and character of government in Barbados. The National Heroes Gallery is an imaginative celebration of the ten National Heroes of Barbados. Among the 10 are Bussa, a slave rebel, Sarah Ann Gill, who campaigned for religious freedom and the cricketer Sir Garfield Sobers. Present-day Bajan artists have created a set of bold abstract sculptures, made from wood, ceramic and metal that represent each Hero.

 *Bridgetown 5d* ✉ Top of Broad Street
National Heroes Gallery and Museum of Parliament: ☎ 310 5400 🕐 Mon–Sat 9–4 💲 Inexpensive

a walk around Bridgetown

Begin at National Heroes Square (➤ 50) and exit the square along St Michael's Row for a look in St Michael's Cathedral (➤ 89).

Continue up St Michael's Row until you reach the gates of Queen's Park (➤ 88).

Stroll through the grounds, peer into the Georgian house, and find the African baobab tree.

Head back to National Heroes Square by the same route and turn right up Marthill Street. The road veers left and then right onto Magazine Lane.

You'll soon come to Synagogue Lane on the left, which leads to the Bridgetown Synagogue (➤ 82) and, behind a low wall to the right of the building, the Jewish cemetery.

Return to Magazine Lane, turning left toward the Montefiore Fountain (➤ 84).

Behind the fountain are the law courts, library and police station. Until they were closed in 1878, the law courts housed the Town Hall Gaol. Behind is Tudor Street, one of the oldest streets in the city.

Continue southwestward along Coleridge Street, turning right onto Swan Street. At the junction (intersection) with Milk Market turn left and continue until you reach the throng of Broad Street.

Once known as New England Street, Broad Street is Bridgetown's main thoroughfare, lined with stores selling

duty-free jewelry, rums, perfumes, leather goods and other goods. An eyecatcher is the pink-and-white Victorian facade of Da Costa's Mall and the dramatic colonial splendor of the Mutual Life Assurance Building at one end of the street.

At this point either take a detour right and stroll along the boardwalk around The Careenage (➤ 83), or continue to the starting point of the walk near the Nelson statue.

Distance Approximately 1.25 miles (2km)
Time 3 hours or half a day with lunch, shopping and rest stops
Start/End Point National Heroes Square ✚ *Bridgetown 5d*
Lunch Waterfront Café ($–$$) ✉ Fairchild Street

QUEEN'S PARK

One of the attractions in the park is the 89ft-high (27m) baobab tree, estimated to be 1,000 years old and believed to have originated in Guinea, West Africa. Its circumference is 82ft (25m). In the pleasant park surrounding the baobab you'll see Barbadians in suits resting for lunch and children playing on the steps of the bandstand. The white Georgian building, Queen's Park House, was once the home of the commander of the British troops. It is now devoted to exhibitions of local arts and the theater.

✚ *Bridgetown 8c* ✉ End of St Michael's Row ⏱ Dawn to dusk ♿ Free
🚌 Fairchild Street

ST MICHAEL'S CATHEDRAL

The cool and tranquil cathedral, also known as the Cathedral Church of St Michael and All Angels, began as a small wooden church with enough seats for a congregation of 100 people. It was built between 1660 and 1665, but was destroyed by a hurricane in 1780 and had to be rebuilt. The new St Michael's became a cathedral when William Hart Coleridge, the first bishop of the island, arrived on Barbados in 1825.

www.stmichaelbarbados.com

✚ *Bridgetown 6d* ✉ St Michael's Row ☎ 427 0790 🕐 Daily 9–5 💲 Free, donations welcome 🚌 Fairchild Street

More to see around Bridgetown

BARBADOS MUSEUM AND HISTORICAL SOCIETY

The Barbados Museum and Historical Society provides a wonderfully old-fashioned introduction to Barbados, housing around 250,000 objects, including West Indian fine and decorative arts, pre-Columbian archaeological pieces and African objects.

Displays begin with the evolution of the planet and a showcase of coral, a major ecosystem of the island. Tools fashioned from coral by the Arawaks and Caribs are here, as are explanations of the tribes' religious beliefs. Fast-forward to the 1600s and you come to the arrival of the English colonists. From 1627 to 1640, until sugar cane flourished, tobacco and cotton were the main crops. Planters relied heavily on African slaves to develop the sugar economy and it is estimated that around 400,000 slaves were imported to Barbados between 1627 and 1807. Their skin was stamped with the initials of their white owner, using an instrument similar to the museum's silver slave-brand dated *c*1800. The museum explains how, after emancipation, slaves tried to make the transition to independent islanders through schooling, farming, entertainment and music.

Outside are examples of the island's architecture and a military gallery. Prints showing the days of slavery, bequeathed to the museum by shipping magnate Sir Edward Cunard, hang in a gallery also graced with shell displays. The African Gallery has recently been redesigned to link the Caribbean with its African ancestry. Of fascinating importance is a collection of rare West Indian books, plus early maps of Barbados, including the earliest known map of the island, dated 1657.

www.barbmuse.org.bb

🚩 2K ✉ St Ann's Garrison, St Michael ☎ 427 0201 🕐 Mon–Sat 9–5, Sun 2–6 ✋ Inexpensive 🍴 Several cafés nearby 🚌 Fairchild Street, or from the south alight at Garrison Savannah ❓ Specially designed tours can be arranged. A Fine Craft Festival is held on the first Sat in Dec

GARRISON HISTORIC AREA

Best places to see ➤ 46–47.

GEORGE WASHINGTON HOUSE

After seven years of fundraising and restoration, the house on Bush Hill where a young George Washington spent seven weeks in 1751 was opened to the public in January 2007. America's first president traveled with his older half-brother, Lawrence, in search of a more temperate climate to help the latter's tuberculosis. The Washingtons also had connections with some of the prominent families on the island.

The two-story Georgian-style house, perched on an escarpment overlooking Carlisle Bay, now serves as a museum and interpretive center and also features a genealogical center, which can help Americans trace their roots on the island. Over the centuries, the building has also served as a private home, a base for French prisoners, offices and part of the British military garrison.

www.georgewashingtonbarbados.org

➕ 2K ✉ Bush Hill, The Garrison, St Michael ☎ 228 5461 🕒 Mon–Fri 9–4:30 💰 Inexpensive 🍴 Café and gift shop on site

MOUNT GAY RUM VISITOR CENTRE

For the rundown on rum and a sip of the neat stuff, visit the Mount Gay Rum Visitor Centre and learn the story of what is reputedly the home of the world's oldest rum (part of Remy-Cointreau since 1989). This is the blending and bottling factory; the distillery itself is in St Lucy, in the north of the island. Step into a traditional-style chattel house and learn about the history of rum since 1703, right up to how it's aged, blended and bottled today. If you book a special luncheon tour with one of the sightseeing operators, or through your resort/hotel rep, then transport, a Bajan buffet and a free miniature bottle of rum are included. You can taste the rum in comfort at the on-site shop. Note how the bottles line wooden shelves behind the bar as they do in rum shops all over the island.

✠ 1J ✉ Brandons, Spring Garden Highway, St Michael ☎ 425 8757
🕐 Daily 9–4:30, tours 9:30 and 3:30 ✋ Moderate 🚌 From Bridgetown,
take the Holetown bus to Brandons

PELICAN CRAFT CENTRE

Between the cruise terminal and Bridgetown,
this small craft center is an interesting stop
if you've decided to walk between the two.
Sitting on land reclaimed from the sea, the
center's pyramidal roofs shelter shops selling
local arts and crafts. It also has workshops
where you can watch some of the island's finest
craftspeople at work. Metalwork, glassware,
wooden crafts, pottery, paintings and batiks
come with a reasonable price tag. You can also buy Royal
Barbados Cigars made by the Caribbean Cigar Company. There
is also a restaurant, and a café serves breakfast, lunch and
afternoon drinks.

✠ 1J ✉ Princess Alice Highway, Bridgetown ☎ 427 5350 🕐 Mon–Fri
10–5, Sat 9–2. Hours are extended during peak holiday season ✋ Free
🍴 Sylvesters ($)

ST PATRICK'S CATHEDRAL

The cornerstone of Roman Catholic St Patrick's Cathedral was originally laid in 1840, but because of lack of funds and too few Catholics, it wasn't consecrated until decades later, in 1899. The interior is dressed with Scottish marble, Irish crests and flags. Nearby, overlooking the Esplanade and Carlisle Bay, is a statue of social reformer and former prime minister Sir Grantley Adams. He stands outside the present government's headquarters and the offices of the prime minister.

✚ 2J ✉ Highway 7, St Michael 🕐 Daily 💵 Free, donations welcome
🍴 Several choices ($–$$) on the coastal road 🚌 Take buses to Bridgetown or the south coast

TYROL COT HERITAGE VILLAGE

Just over 2.5 acres (1ha) of landscaped gardens encompass Tyrol Cot Heritage Village, said to be the birthplace of Barbadian democracy. Built in 1854, the house was home to the late Sir Grantley Adams, founder of the Barbados Labor Party, from 1929. He was the first premier of Barbados and the only prime minister of the short-lived West Indies Federation. Adams was one of the 10 national heroes named by the present prime minister, who also declared Adams's birthdate (April 28, 1898) National Heroes Day and a public holiday. Adams's son, Tom, who became prime

minister from 1976 to 1985, was born here. Restored by the Barbados National Trust, the house is built of coral stone blocks. Inside it still has the Adams's own Barbadian antique furniture. Within the

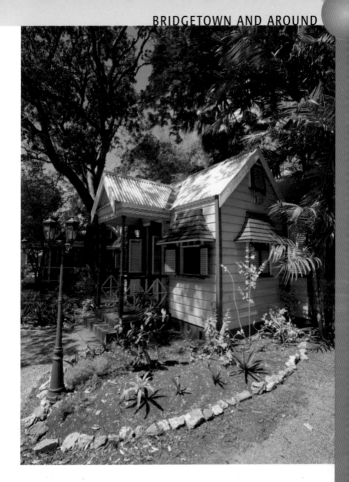

4-acre (1.5-ha) grounds is a craft village in the style of a traditional chattel house settlement – the moveable homes of plantation workers. You can buy handmade souvenirs by local artists here. There is a replica of an 1820s thatched slave hut revealing the simple way slaves lived in the days of the great sugar plantations.

✚ 2J ✉ Codrington Hill, St Michael ☎ 424 2074 🕐 Mon–Fri 9–5; shops may close earlier 👍 Inexpensive 🍴 The Rum Shop, on site 🚌 From Bridgetown, take the Cave Hill, Holders Green or Jackson bus

NB: See also Southern Barbados listings (➤ 146–153) for additional establishments in St Michael and Christ Church.

HOTELS

▼▼ ▼▼ Hilton Barbados ($$$)

This 350-room Hilton resort is 1 mile (1.5km) from the center of Bridgetown, on the beach. It has an impressive lagoon pool, children's club, tennis courts and three restaurants, including the prestigious restaurant The Grille.

✉ Needham's Point, St Michael ☎ 426 0200; www.hiltoncaribbean.com

▼▼▼ The Savannah ($$$)

Two hundred years old, directly on the beach at Hastings, the hotel is part of the "Gems of Barbados" group and has luxurious rooms, with mahogany four-poster beds. Go for the beachfront suites. Ten minutes from downtown Bridgetown and within walking distance of Garrison Savannah.

✉ Hastings, Christ Church ☎ 435 9473; www.gemsbarbados.com

RESTAURANTS

▼▼ Brown Sugar ($$–$$$)

See page 58.

▼▼▼ Champers ($$–$$$)

Set on the water's edge of Hastings, this popular wine bar and restaurant has a bistro downstairs and a pleasant dining room upstairs boasting fine views of the ocean.

✉ Skeetes Hill, Hastings, Christ Church ☎ 434 3463; www.champersbarbados.com 🕔 Daily lunch and dinner

▼▼▼ The Grille ($$$)

Elegant a la carte restaurant at the Hilton, Barbados, serving modern Caribbean dishes and specializing in top-quality grilled meat and fish. The beautiful dining room is ornamented with fine drapes and lit with intimate spotlight table lights and chandeliers.

✉ Needham's Point, St Michael ☎ 426 0200; www.hiltoncaribbean.com 🕔 Tue–Sat 6:30pm–10pm

Lobster Alive ($$)
Live spiny lobsters, flown in from Bequia and kept in a large tank, are the feature of this cheerful restaurant. Sunbeds, umbrellas and showers are provided for customers. Live jazz three times a week.
✉ Wesley House, Bay Street, Bridgetown ☎ 435 0305; www.lobsteralive.net 🕓 Mon–Sat lunch and dinner, Sun lunch only

Wispers on the Bay ($$$)
Award-winning dining with a romantic atmosphere, right on the beach. A three-course, fixed-price dinner menu features international new-wave cuisine, cooked with imaginative flair and beautifully presented.
✉ Old Bayshore Complex, Bay Street, Bridgetown ☎ 826 5222; www.wispersonthebay.com 🕓 Mon–Sat lunch and dinner

SHOPPING

Cave Shepherd
Famous Bajan department store with a wide selection of beachwear, souvenirs and household items.
✉ Broad Street, Bridgetown ☎ 227 2121; www.caveshepherd.com 🕓 Mon–Sat 9–5

Earth Mother Botanicals
Soap, shampoo and other beauty products made from local organic ingredients including guava, bay rum and morinda leaf.
✉ Pelican Craft Centre 🕓 228 2743 🕓 Mon–Fri 9–6, Sat 9–1

Kirby Gallery
A good place to pick up original art and limited-edition prints by local and international artists.
✉ The Courtyard, Hastings, Christ Church ☎ 430 3032; www.kirbyartgallery.com 🕓 Mon–Fri 9–1, 2–5

Market
The Saturday morning Cheapside Fruit Market (Lower Broad Street, Bridgetown) offers a colorful display of fruit, handicrafts, jewelry and Rastafarian curios.

Medford Craft World

Sculptures created from Barbados mahogany with a unique finish. The showroom has a wide range of local crafts.

✉ Whitehall Main Road, St Michael ☎ 425 1919 🕙 Mon–Fri 8–5, Sat 9–1

Women's Self Help Shop

Home-made Barbadian sweets, preserves, pepper sauce and craft objects. The shop is part of the Women's Self Help organization that supports local women and their small enterprises.

✉ Royal Bank Building, Broad Street ☎ 426 2570 🕙 Mon–Fri 9–5, Sat 9–1

ENTERTAINMENT

The Boatyard

Beach club with water sports including sea trampolines and water slides. Sharkeys Bar gets busy after dark with DJs and cocktails.

✉ Bay Street, St Michael ☎ 436 2622; www.theboatyard.com 🕙 Daily 10–2

Harbour Lights

Massively popular beach-front club. Dance under the stars or indoors. The only nightspot where beachwear is acceptable.

✉ Bay Street, St Michael ☎ 436 7225; www.harbourlightsbarbados.com 🕙 Mon, Wed, Fri 7–3

Harbour Master Cruises

See page 62.

SPORT AND ACTIVITIES

Kensington Oval

Try to catch a live cricket match: the regional season runs January to March, while the international season is April to May.

✉ Kensington Oval, Bridgetown ☎ 436 1397

Silver Moon

Upmarket catamaran cruise with a free bar and lunchtime buffet on board.

✉ The Careenage, Bridgetown ☎ 438 2088; www.silvermoonbarbados.com

Northern Barbados

In contrast to the south, the far north of the island is sleepy and undeveloped, covered with rippling sugar-cane fields sloping down to small settlements on sandy beaches, or, in the far north, craggy cliffs.

Speightstown

Holetown

This is where the warm Caribbean meets the stormy, rough Atlantic Ocean. The scenery is reminiscent of how Barbados may have looked 100 years ago before tourism developed: goats and sheep in the fields, unassuming, often ramshackle little houses, many churches, the occasional rum shack and, to the east, the wilder Scotland District, which almost resembles the moorlands and rolling hills after which it is named.

AERIEL TREK

Right in the middle of
Barbados is an adrenaline
junkie's dream. High over a
deep rainforest gully eight zip-
lines, or wire cables, run
between giant ancient trees.
Once strapped into a safety
harness by helpful and
informed guides, willing
victims are attached to the
zip-line and before you've
time to think, whoosh! You've
arrived at the other side,
having flown over the lush
green foliage below.
At each platform or stop,
guides explain a little about
the flora and fauna of the
forest – the age and type
of tree, the formation of
the gully, what plants and
nuts are used for. It's a
thrilling ride, though not for
the faint-hearted. It's also
possible to go on a nature
trek along the bottom of the
gully with a rope-assisted
descent into a deep cavern.

✚ 3G ✉ Jack-in-the-Box Gully,
Walkes Spring St Thomas ☎ 433
8735; www.aerialtrek.com
🕘 Daily 9–2:30 ✋ Moderate
🚐 Pick-up from hotels available

ANDROMEDA BOTANIC GARDENS

Best places to see ➤ 36–37.

ANIMAL FLOWER CAVE

The cave is at North Point, unsurprisingly as far north as you can go on Barbados. When you visit you can expect a breezy and exposed, yet fabulous, spot for photography. A flight of steps leads down to a cavern carved out of the coral rock where there are scattered pools containing hundreds of sea anemones. Natural historian Griffith Hughes described them as animal flowers in 1750. Look behind you and the view of the ocean is amazing. Look down and you'll see the pools are deep enough to swim in, but be careful of the slippery surface.

✚ 2C ✉ St Lucy ☎ 439 8797 🕔 Daily 9–5 ✋ Inexpensive 🍴 Café ($) serving snacks 🚌 From Bridgetown take the Connell town bus

ARLINGTON HOUSE

Arlington House is a beautifully restored 18th-century building in the middle of Speightstown. It was occupied by the Skinner family, highly successful shipping merchants, for 200 years. The ground floor was originally a ship's chandlery that would have served the once bustling port of Speightstown.

Now Arlington House is a wonderful small museum that brings to life the history and culture of northern Barbados in a captivating fashion. There are three floors, each with a different themed exhibition showing the history and culture of Barbados in an imaginative way. The ground floor introduces visitors to the sounds and characters of Speightstown, past and present, with audio-visual displays and old photographs. You'll meet the coconut man and local businessmen and hear the cries of market vendors. The first floor has two displays. One is a collection of old maps, including the room-sized 1820 Bowen Map of Barbados. The second is a fascinating insight into Plantation life in Barbados: the display features a dramatic reconstruction of the end of slavery, and gives details of the daily lives of the workers and owners of the many sugar plantations once on the island that gave rise to Barbados being called the "richest spote of lande in the worlde." The third floor is aimed at entertaining children with a reconstructed jetty and interactive exhibits, including a talking pirate and virtual turtles that swim round the room.

🚹 1E ✉ Queen Street, Speightstown ☎ 422 4064 🕐 Mon–Fri 10–5, Sat 10–3 ✋ Inexpensive 🍽 Cafés in Speightstown 🚌 Buses from all over the island

BATHSHEBA

Best places to see ➤ 40–41.

BARBADOS POLO CLUB

Polo on the island dates back to the 1900s and was introduced by the British cavalry who, having tired of playing against each other, roped in the locals. The Barbados Polo Club was established at what is now the historic Garrison in Bridgetown in 1929 and moved in the 1960s to its current location on Holders Hill in St James, with its wide grassland and towering trees. Recently, three new polo fields have been developed. Each year, between October and the end of May, the season's itinerary includes fixtures against international teams, bolstered by Bajan hospitality. These matches are well attended by tourists, many of whom regard polo as one of the most vibrant sports on the island. Afternoon tea and cucumber sandwiches are served in style in the atmospheric wooden clubhouse after the game.

✚ 1H ✉ Holders Hill, St James ☎ 432 1802; www.barbadospoloclub.com
✋ Free, but priced tickets for international matches

BARBADOS WILDLIFE RESERVE

Best places to see ➤ 38–39.

a drive along East Coast Road

The East Coast Road (also called the Ernie Bourne Highway) runs through the parishes of St Andrew and St Joseph between the Atlantic Ocean and the Scotland District. Opened in 1966 by Queen Elizabeth II, the road slithers along the route of the old railroad from Bridgetown to Belleplaine and passes three of our Best Places to See.

Have your hotel prepare a picnic lunch beforehand so you can stop and spend an hour sitting on the sands and watching the surfers. Remember, it is too dangerous for swimming, but at low tide you can explore the rock pools.

Start from Bathsheba (▶ 40). Spend a while at Andromeda Botanic Gardens (▶ 36) and Bathsheba village before heading north, keeping the ocean to your right.

Worn, wooden chattel houses face deserted beaches scattered with rock formations and giant boulders. Next comes Cattlewash (▶ 40). The road here is not busy, so you can stop at intervals to take photographs. The Scotland District on your left, so called because it reminded British settlers of the Scottish Highlands, is a rugged area of steep lanes with sheep and cattle grazing on the hillsides. Many potters exploit the clay deposits in this area (▶ 42).

Drive on a little farther to reach a peaceful resting spot, Barclays Park, a picnic area popular with locals on public holidays. On weekdays, you might be the only visitor. The park was a gift from Barclays Bank in 1966, the year of independence.

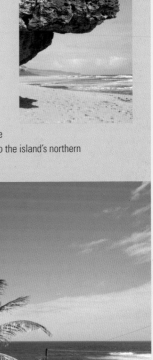

This short drive finishes up at the village of Belleplaine, where the railroad once terminated.

Distance 4 miles (6.5km)
Time Half a day with lunch and stops
Start Point Bathsheba ✚ 4F
End Point Belleplaine ✚ 3E
Lunch Take a picnic or have a tasty Bajan lunch at Sand Dunes Restaurant close to Belleplaine Village ❓ The drive can be done in reverse and linked with part of the drive to the island's northern tip (➤ 118).

CHALKY MOUNT POTTERIES

Best places to see ➤ 42–43.

EARTHWORKS POTTERY

Earthworks Pottery is another showcase for Barbadian art crafted from local clay. Founded in 1983 as a small art studio making individual pieces, the pottery has expanded and now produces a range of trinket bowls, carvings and custom-made tiles. It's a bright and cheerful place where practically everything except the trees and grass are painted. There's also a batik studio and an art gallery. After touring the pottery and watching the artists at work, you can dine on light meals outside on the veranda next to a bamboo patch.

www.earthworks-pottery.com

✚ 2G ✉ Edgehill, St Thomas ☎ 425 0223 🕒 Mon–Fri 9–5, Sat 9–1 (except public hols) 🎟 Free 🍴 Treehouse Café ($–$$, ☎ 425 0223) 🚍 From Bridgetown, take Hillaby or Shop Hill bus

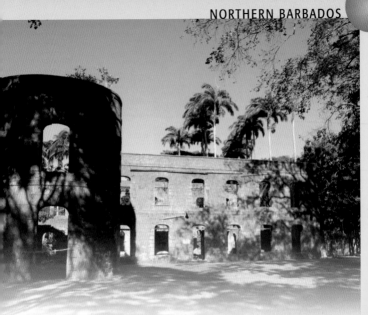

FARLEY HILL NATIONAL PARK

Once the most imposing mansion on Barbados, 19th-century Farley Hill at Farley Hill National Park was built to show off the accumulated wealth of the sugar planters. Originally known as Grenade Hall, it came into the hands of Sir Thomas Graham Briggs, who named it Farley Hill. Amid the fire-damaged ruins, overgrown with plants, you can imagine the sumptuous parties held here during the heyday of the sugar boom. Prince Alfred, the second son of Queen Victoria, and Prince George (later George V of England) arrived in carriages to take luncheon or dinner. Though you can't enter the roofless house for safety reasons, you can get a good look at the ruins through its windowless frames. It makes a dramatic setting for outdoor jazz at the annual Barbados Jazz Festival in January. The park trail leads to a picnic spot overlooking the Scotland District and Atlantic coastline, where you might hear the rustle of green monkeys in the treetops above.

🚻 2E ✉ St Peter ☎ 422 3555 🕐 Daily 8:30–6 💲 Inexpensive 🍴 Take a picnic and eat in the grounds 🚌 From Bridgetown, Speightstown and Bathsheba

FAIRMONT ROYAL PAVILION ESTATE

The west coast has many pseudonyms, "Platinum Coast," "Gold Coast" and even "Millionaires' Row," maybe because its sands are silvery or gold, and the hotels ultra-glamorous and extremely expensive. Commanding an historic estate is the Fairmont Royal Pavilion, where writers meet their publishers and where Sir Edward Cunard, one of the world's greatest shipping magnates, lived.

Renowned South American-born landscape architect Fernando Tabora created the tropical gardens here. There is a weekly guided botanic tour of the courtyards, beds and lily ponds on Wednesdays at 10am. You follow the head gardener through more than 400 coconut trees. If you're stylishly dressed, you can take afternoon tea in the Café Taboras of the Royal Pavilion. In traditional 1930s manner, a white pot of Earl Grey, Darjeeling, peppermint or camomile tea is brought to your table, accompanied by a tiered stand of chocolate brownies, pastries, jam turnovers and crustless cucumber sandwiches.

➕ 1F ✉ Porters, St James ☎ 422 5555 🕐 Tour at 10am Wed
🍴 Afternoon tea daily 3:30–5 🚌 From Bridgetown or Speightstown

FOLKESTONE MARINE RESERVE

Not solely of interest to scuba divers, the park tells the story of the marine life of the island through its museum. Here you'll learn interesting snippets of information, such as the fact that the sex of a sea turtle is determined by the temperature of the sand the eggs are laid in. Then rent some equipment and go snorkeling in the sea to see fish, sponges and coral. Nearby, glass-bottomed boat tours will take you out to Dottins Reef wrecks and the reefs.

🚩 1G ✉ Folkestone, St James ☎ 425 1200 🕐 Park open daily, museum Mon–Fri 9:30–5, Sat–Sun 10–6 ✋ Park free, museum inexpensive 🍴 Beach bars, cafés and a picnic area 🚌 From Speightstown, Holetown and Bridgetown

FRANK HUTSON SUGAR MUSEUM

Yet another property run by the Barbados National Trust is the Frank Hutson Sugar Museum. Its fascinating collection of old sugar objects and machinery tells the story of what was formerly the most prized commodity on the island. The collection was started by Barbadian engineer Sir Frank Hutson and is a tribute to his passion. During the cane-grinding season, which runs from February to May, you can pay a visit to the boiling house at the Portvale Sugar Factory, one of only a few factories that are still working on the island, for a dollop of molasses.

✚ 2G ✉ St James ☎ 426 2421 ⏱ Mon–Sat 9–5 (except public hols) ✋ Museum inexpensive; factory tour extra 🍴 Excellent cafés ($–$$) on the coast road 🚌 From Bridgetown take the Rock Hall bus

GRENADE HALL FOREST AND SIGNAL STATION

This is a good place to escape the relentless Caribbean sun. A trail descends through a web of vines and winds on for nearly a mile on paved paths smothered in moss. It's slippery, so wear strong soles with treads.

At intervals you'll see questions (forming part of a quiz), plus quotes and anecdotes from the likes of Charles Darwin and an Amerindian chief. These remind us that humans continue to exploit the rainforests of the world for timber. There is a cave that sheltered Arawak Indians and, later, Rastafarians and escaped convicts. Shell tools found here are on display at the Barbados Wildlife Reserve (➤ 38).

Next door to the forest is the restored, whitewashed tower of the Grenade Hall Signal Station, built in 1819. Barbados had a string of such stations, established following the slave rebellion of 1816. During the uprising, one-fifth of the island's sugar-cane fields was set on fire and scores of slaves were killed, executed or deported. The news of the revolt took hours to reach the authorities in Bridgetown, so the following year the governor proposed that a chain of signal stations be built to aid communication. The network relayed messages by flags, to which watchful messengers responded by dispatching the news to headquarters in Bridgetown. Following the abolition of slavery, the signal stations' crews passed the time by monitoring approaching cargo ships and announcing school times. An audio tape plays as you browse through displays of clay pipe fragments and musket balls. Climb the polished wooden staircase to the lookout at the top and imagine life before the telephone.

✚ 2E ✉ Farley Hill, St Peter ☎ 422 8826 🕐 Daily 10–5, last entry 3:30–3:45 (arrive before 3 to see the monkeys) 🖐 Moderate; includes Forest and Signal Station 🚌 From Speightstown

HARRISON'S CAVE

Best places to see ➤ 48–49.

HOLETOWN

You can spend a full day in Holetown or, during February, a full week at the annual Holetown Festival. The festival coincides with the landing of the first British settlers to the island on February 17, 1627. Prior to this, English Captain John Powell, sailing the *Olive Blossom* to Brazil, anchored off the small natural harbor and set foot at what he declared Jamestown. Later, the settlement was

renamed "the Hole" after a tiny inlet where boats could harbor. Back in England, Powell reported his discovery to his employer, Sir William Courteen, an Anglo-Dutch merchant. Courteen responded by sending out an expedition of about 80 settlers and a group of African slaves captured from a Spanish galleon. Powell headed the mission, sailing the *William and John*. More white settlers followed, setting up home and establishing crops of cotton, ginger and tobacco. They soon found out how to tend and utilize the soil using methods taught to them by Arawak Indians brought over especially from Guyana. Commemorating the landing is the Holetown Monument on the forecourt of the town's police station, the former fort. The date, for some reason, mistakenly reads 1605.

Around the town are a few buildings dating from the 17th century. St James was the first church, originally built of wood. Inside is the old font and a bell inscribed "God Bless King William, 1696." Modern gems include the exceptional Patisserie Flindt (➤ 59), plus a chattel village of craft shops and an art gallery.

🚩 1G ✉ St James 🍴 Excellent cafés and bars ($–$$) 🚌 From Bridgetown, Speightstown and Bathsheba

HUNTE'S GARDENS

On the edge of his property in Castle Grant (a small settlement mid-island between Holetown and Bathsheba) Antony Hunte, a local horticulturist who has sold plants and garden accessories for many years, has created a staggeringly beautiful garden in a deep gully. A winding staircase descends 30ft (9m) to the gully floor past terraced beds crammed full of tropical shrubs and blooms – tall cabbage palms, water hyacinths, jade-green alocasias, purple-black colocasias and feathery phoenix robellini, crotons, bromeliads and orchids. The garden is interlaced with pretty Italian statues and tables and chairs are laid out in cool shady spots for a bit of respite from the Caribbean heat. Ever the showman, Antony often plays soaring opera and classical music that floats out over the gardens and entertains visitors, after they've strolled through the gully, while they enjoy a teapot of rum punch on his elegant verandah. Come to admire his artistry, to buy tropical plants in the nursery or just to relax among the ancient palm and breadfruit trees.

✚ 3G ✉ Castle Grant, St Joseph ☎ 433 3333 🕓 Daily 9–4
✋ Moderate ❓ To find the garden follow the red and white signs that are all over the island

MORGAN LEWIS SUGAR MILL

At one time Barbados had many wind-driven mills. They were introduced by the Dutch planters from Brazil when they brought sugar cane to the island in the 1600s, flattening the forests to make way for vast plantations worked by slaves from Africa. The mills crushed the sugar cane to extract the juice, which would then go through a process of boiling and cooling before finally ending up as sugar for export. Built around 1776, the restored Morgan Lewis Sugar Mill is the largest complete windmill in the Caribbean. It is set within a working farm and occupies a gorgeous location, flanked by a row of mahogany trees. Inside is the grinding machinery, made by a firm in Derby, England. Although not as vital as tourism, the sugar industry is still important to Barbados.

✚ 2D ✉ Near Cherry Tree Hill, St Andrew ☎ 422 9213
🕐 Tue–Sat 8–4 ✋ Moderate

ST NICHOLAS ABBEY

Just beyond the magnificent lookout of Cherry Tree Hill in St Andrew, St Nicholas Abbey is a wonderful, Jacobean-style plantation house, believed to be one of only three still standing in the western hemisphere and recently beautifully renovated. The house was built in 1650 and is supposedly the oldest in Barbados, although it was never an abbey. During the days of slavery, it was a working sugar plantation. Its past is riddled with scandal: the original owner, Colonel Benjamin Berringer, was killed in a duel with his neighbor, John Yeamans, after Yeamans had an affair with Berringer's wife. Yeamans then married the wife but the two fled the island in 1669 for Carolina, unable to cope with the prejudices of the day, and Yeamans became governor of the colony after only three years.

Guided tours of the ground floor allow visitors to see the cedar paneling, Dutch gables and Chinese Chippendale staircase.

www.stnicholasabbey.com

🚩 2D 📧 Cherry Tree Hill, St Peter

☎ 422 8725 🕔 Daily 10–3:30

🍴 Café ($) ✋ Expensive

SIX MEN'S BAY

At the coastal village of Six Men's Bay wooden fishing boats, waiting to be treated or repaired, are pulled up onto the grass beyond the shoreline. Nets and floats lie scattered about, as do chunks of mahogany used by boatbuilders to make the keels. If you're lucky, you might see work being carried out. Usually the boatbuilders don't mind if you stop to chat or ask questions. Pretty wooden houses line one side of the road while the sea laps the sands opposite, making this a refreshing place to rest before reaching Speightstown.

🚩 1E 📧 Near Speightstown

🍴 Restaurants in Speightstown ($–$$)

🚌 Speightstown bus from Bridgetown

a drive to the island's northern tip

This drive covers the northern tip of the island, from the parish of St Peter up to St Lucy.

Head north on the coastal road out of Speightstown, keeping the sea to your left. Pass the entrance to Almond Beach Village and Port St Charles Marina and turn right up a hill. Continue over the junction (intersection) and look out for All Saints Church.

Flanked by sugar-cane fields, All Saints Church, built in 1649, is the resting place of William Arnold, the first English settler. His grave is clearly marked.

Continue to a T-junction (intersection), turn right and follow signs to the Barbados Wildlife Reserve (▶ 38).

Farley Hill National Park (► 107) appears first, to your left. Park inside and walk around the ruins. Leave the car where it is and cross the road to the Barbados Wildlife Reserve. After seeing the animals, birds and reptiles, have a refreshing drink in the Mahogany Bar before exploring nearby Grenade Hall Forest and Signal Station (► 112).

Leave Farley Hill and follow signs to the Morgan Lewis Sugar Mill (► 116) and Cherry Tree Hill. Stop by St Nicholas Abbey, the island's oldest house. You can then loop back to the main road into St Lucy and onto the Animal Flower Cave (► 101) and North Point.

At stunning North Point take tea and photos until it's time to head back on the coastal road to Speightstown.

Distance Approx 16 miles (26km)
Time Half a day with lunch, to a full day
Start/End Point Speightstown ✚ 1E
Lunch St Nicholas Abbey Café ($$) ❓ If you plan to walk the forest nature trail, wear sturdy shoes and be careful on the mossy paths

SPEIGHTSTOWN

Best places to see ➤ 52–53.

SPRINGVALE ECO-HERITAGE MUSEUM (SPRINGVALE PLANTATION)

The small planters' house on this former sugar plantation has been turned into an interesting museum, full of artefacts from days gone. Wall displays and accurately dressed figures explain the daily chores of working people in Barbados, post slavery. There's the washerwoman with her board, the hawker in her broad-rimmed hat and apron who shouted "look me here" to attract attention, and the basket-maker who fetched vines out of local ravines to twist into containers. Collections of mahogany furniture, clay pots and kitchen implements are artfully exhibited. Newlands Greenidge, the plantation's owner, is a highly enthusiastic guide with a wealth of information about the history of ordinary lives in Barbados. He's usually on hand to take visitors for a walk through the plantation gardens, pointing out each and every plant and its medicinal or other uses. On site there's also the Gang of Four studio where Antiguan artist Gordon Webster works and sells his vividly colored abstract paintings.

✚ 3F ✉ Springvale, Highway 2, St Andrew ☎ 437 9400

🕐 Mon–Sat 10–4

💆 Inexpensive

WELCHMAN HALL GULLY

Formed by a series of caves that collapsed, the gully is a 0.6-mile (1km) corridor of tropical jungle cutting through the coral foundations of the island. Cliffs rise up on either side, and banana, nutmeg and fig trees are among the 200 or so species of tropical plant that grow in the gully. It is said to take its name from a Welsh settler called Williams who once owned the land through which the ravine cuts. His descendants planted some of the trees. The National Trust, which takes care of the site, has added a few plants but it's mostly left in a wild state. As you walk through it's easy to imagine how Barbados must have looked before the first settlers arrived and carried out a program of ravaging deforestation. At one end a stalactite and stalagmite have met in the middle to form a 46in (118cm) diameter column that appears to hold up the cliff. Around dawn or dusk you might spot Barbados green monkeys.

www.welchmanhallgullybarbados.com

🚭 2G 🖂 St Thomas ☎ 438 6671 🕐 Daily 9–5 (except public hols) 🍴 View Point Restaurant opposite 👤 Moderate 🚌 From Bridgetown take the Sturges bus ❓ Wear good walking shoes and take drinking water

a walk along the Arbib Nature and Heritage Trail

The Arbib Nature and Heritage Trail – run by the Barbados National Trust – won the Caribbean ecotourism award, beating entrants from 20 other islands. There are two trails of varying length: the longer "Whim Adventure" trail cuts through the Whim Gully, one of many ravines of limestone and coral that lead to the sea and drain the island's rainfall. Get the most from the trail by taking a guided walk.

The trail begins from Speightstown (although it isn't well marked) and passes villages, sugar-cane plantations and cottonfields. As you go, the guide stops to point out herbs and other plants that have medicinal uses, such

as the castor-oil plant. You will weave through mango, banana and grapefruit trees, dog's dumpling, breadfruit, the bearded fig and a pumpkin patch.

In the interior villages you'll see Barbadian chattel houses (the traditional homes of plantation workers), some with their own kitchen gardens. The chattel is built perfectly symmetrically with a door in the center and windows either side. Traditionally the roof is made of shingle, with a steep pitch to allow rain to run off easily. Surprisingly, these tiny buildings withstand hurricanes pretty well, too.

As the walk nears the coast, the houses become grander. You can rest near the cannon at the remains of 18th-century Dover Fort, overlooking the water-front apartments of Port St Charles, before heading back to Speightstown. Stroll back along the sandy beach in front of the Almond Beach Village before joining your guide for a drink at the rum shop at Speightstown harborside.

Distance 5 miles (8km); alternative 3.5-mile (5.5km) trail
Time 2 to 3.5 hours, depending on stops
Start/End Point Speightstown ✚ 1E
Lunch Various places in Speightstown ($–$$)
❓ Walks operate Wed, Thu, Sat at 9:30 and 2:30 and must be reserved. Wear proper walking shoes, a sun hat, sunscreen and take drinking water (☎ 426 2421)

HOTELS

⏴⏴ Almond Beach Club and Spa ($$)

Luxurious, adults-only all-inclusive on the west coast in a romantic setting, with a lavish spa; a grown-up alternative to the family Almond Beach Village farther north.

✉ Vauxhall, St James ☎ 432 7840; www.almondresorts.com

⏴⏴⏴ Almond Beach Village ($$–$$$)

An all-inclusive resort consisting of 395 rooms and suites within a historic sugar plantation, originally built in 1865, close to the sea. Ideal for families, with a spa, fitness classes, tennis and golf lessons, and masses of children's facilities (▶ 74).

✉ St Peter, Speightstown ☎ 422 4900; www.almondresorts.com

⏴⏴⏴ Cobblers Cove ($$$)

Pink turrets rising from manicured, tropical green foliage distinguish this Relais et Chateaux property perched above coral sands. Cottages and suites, furnished with cottons and rattan furniture, open onto gardens or the sea. The ultimate, though, is a seafront suite with rooftop plunge pool (▶ 74).

✉ St Peter, Speightstown ☎ 422 2291; www.cobblerscove.com

⏴⏴⏴⏴ Colony Club ($$$)

A former gentleman's club, the Colony is now a sophisticated hotel with an old Englishness and charm catering to both couples and families. Extensive tropical gardens with four freshwater pools.

✉ Porters, St James ☎ 422 2335; www.colonyclubhotel.com

⏴⏴⏴⏴ Coral Reef Club ($$)

A family-run and owned hotel that offers great service and fine dining in a colonial plantation setting. Both garden and beach are among the loveliest on the island (▶ 74).

✉ St James ☎ 422 2372 (booking agent); www.coralreefbarbados.com

⏴⏴ Discovery Bay by Rex Resorts ($$)

Popular all-inclusive in a charming old plantation-style property at the northern end of Speightstown. Friendly staff, an old-fashioned atmosphere and excellent value for money mean that guests return again and again. Rooms are spacious with tv, tea/coffee makers and free wifi. Secluded gardens, beachfront position and a large pool on site (➤ 75).

✉ Holetown, St James ☎ 432 1301; www.rexresorts.com

▼▼ ▼▼ Fairmont Royal Pavilion Hotel ($$$)

Although a beachfront resort, this rose-pink, graceful top-price establishment is very private. It is shrouded in tropical gardens so diverse that it takes a botanical tour (held weekly) to explain the species. Enjoy the afternoon tea of cakes and cucumber sandwiches, served in a traditional, 1930s English style (➤ 75).

✉ Porters, St James ☎ 422 5555; www.fairmont.com

▼▼ Little Good Harbour ($$$)

Classy boutique hotel with a handful of attractive guest cottages on a peaceful stretch of coast and the renowned Fishpot restaurant on site. Self-catering units have fully equipped kitchens and one, two or three bedrooms.

✉ Shermans, St Peter ☎ 439 3000; www.littlegoodharbourbarbados.com

▼▼ New Edgewater Hotel ($$)

Set on a ledge overlooking the Atlantic crashing onto rock formations below, the New Edgewater, one of the few hotels on the east coast, is only a few steps from Bathsheba beach. Voted Best Small Hotel by readers of *Caribbean Life* magazine. Ideal for experienced surfers or anybody looking for a quiet, relaxed, glitz-free vacation.

✉ Bathsheba beach ☎ 433 9900; www.newedgewater.com

▼▼▼ The Sandpiper ($$)

Just 20 minutes from Bridgetown in Holetown, this charming beachfront hotel, set amid landscaped grounds, offers individual suites for families and couples. Facilities include a top-class restaurant, pool, tennis and water sports. Member of the Small Luxury Hotels of the World (➤ 75).

✉ Holetown, St James ☎ 422 2251; www.sandpiperbarbados.com

▽▽▽▽ Sandy Lane ($$$)

Unashamed luxury, this famous hotel has accommodated royalty and movie stars in its luxurious rooms and suites since 1961. The Palladian-style cream coral stone buildings are situated in a beautiful 800-acre (324ha) beachfront estate (➤ 75).

✉ St James ☎ 444 2000; www.sandylane.com

▽▽▽ Treasure Beach ($$)

Boutique hotel set in lush tropical gardens right by a white sand beach (➤ 75). Intimate and friendly atmosphere and an excellent poolside restaurant.

✉ Paynes Bay, St James ☎ 432 1346; www.treasurebeachhotel.com

RESTAURANTS

▽▽▽ Al Fresco ($$)
See page 58.

Cariba ($$$)

Top British chef Glen Bent runs this tiny side-street eatery with his wife, who creates a warm atmosphere. The cooking is superb and unique dishes are a mix of modern Caribbean and Asian flavors.

✉ 1 Clarke's Gap, Derricks, St James ☎ 432 8737 ⏱ Mon–Sat 6pm–9:30pm

Cassareep ($)

Cheerful and stylish lunchtime café overlooking the water with a range of wraps, sandwiches and salads. Dinner menus are Middle Eastern with dips, kebabs and spicy stews.

✉ Seaside, Speightstown, St Peter ☎ 422 3573; cassareep.net ⏱ Mon–Sat 9–6, also Thu, Fri, Sat 7–10

▽▽▽▽ The Cliff ($$$)

Regarded as the finest, most expensive and most exclusive restaurant on the island, The Cliff has a neoclassical, tiered dining terrace overlooking the sea. Each dish is a masterpiece. Booked up for months in advance.

✉ Derricks, St James ☎ 432 1922; www.thecliffbarbados.com ⏱ Mon–Sat 6:30pm–9:30pm

▼▼▼ Daphne's ($$$)

Grilled specials and seafoods with an Italian influence are featured at this elegant contemporary restaurant, sister to Daphne's in London. Famous cocktails and an extensive wine list.

✉ Payne's Bay ☎ 432 2731; www.daphnesbarbados.com ⏰ Daily 12:30–3, 6:30–10:30

The Fish Pot ($$)

A regular haunt in the north for A-list celebrities who dine at this restaurant in part of a converted fort on the beach. As the name suggests, there's a fish-oriented menu.

✉ Little Good Harbour, Sherman's ☎ 439 3000 ⏰ Daily lunch and dinner

▼▼▼ Lone Star Restaurant and Hotel ($$–$$$)

Stylish beach restaurant offering eclectic Mediterranean, modern European and traditional Caribbean dishes, from meze to curries, served al fresco (➤ 75).

✉ Mount Standfast, St James ☎ 419 0599; www.thelonestar.com ⏰ Daily 11:30–3:30, 6–10

▼▼▼ Mango's By the Sea ($$)

Romantic setting overlooking the ocean and known for its lobster bisque and grilled lobster. Also serves New York strip steak and barbecued back ribs, followed by home-made desserts and excellent espresso.

✉ By the sea, Speightstown, St Peter ☎ 422 0704; www.mangosbythesea.com ⏰ Daily 6pm–9:45pm

▼▼▼ Mullins ($$–$$$)

See page 58.

Naniki ($$)

Staggering views over the coast accompany fresh Caribbean cuisine and charming service in a friendly atmosphere. Off the beaten track in a tranquil and relaxing spot. Sunday brunch is accompanied by live jazz.

✉ Surinam, St Joseph ☎ 433 1300; www.lushlife.bb ⏰ Daily lunch only

Patisserie Flindt ($$)
See page 59.

Round House Inn & Bar ($)
Sandwiches, soups, quiches and seafood, Monday to Saturday.
Take in the great views with your lunch. Live acoustic guitar on
Sunday lunchtimes and jazz on Wednesday evenings.
✉ Bathsheba ☎ 433 9678; www.roundhousebarbados.com ⏰ Mon–Sat
8am–9:30pm

♛♛ Scarlet ($$)
Best known for its funky red interior with pop art decor and an
extensive range of delicious cocktails. Buzzing atmosphere and
eclectic food with Italian, Caribbean and Asian influences. Popular
with pre- and post-dinner crowd.
✉ Paynes Bay, St James ☎ 432 3663 ⏰ Tue–Sun 5pm–late

♛♛ Il Tempio ($$)
Traditional Italian cuisine in a romantic beach setting. Given the seal
of approval by Italian holidaymakers, including the late Pavarotti.
✉ Fitts Village, St James ☎ 417 0057; www.iltempiorestaurant.com
⏰ Tue–Sun 12–2:30, 6:30–10; closed Aug and Sep

The Terrace Restaurant ($$$)
A well-recommended Relais et Chateaux restaurant within
Cobblers Cove Hotel. Continental food with a Caribbean accent is
prepared by French-trained chefs and served on a romantic terrace
by the sea. Friday night is a fish and caviar extravaganza. Great
cocktails and a renowned wine list are highlights. Reservations
are essential.
✉ Cobblers Cove, St Peter ☎ 422 2291; www.cobblerscove.com ⏰ Daily
12:30–2:30, 6:30–9

♛♛♛ The Tides ($$$)
Set on the water's edge overlooking the sea with an excellent
menu of chowders, salads, pasta, seafood and the fresh catch of
the day; there's also an imaginative vegetarian menu. Try the

bistro-style restaurant inside for casual dining or the terrace outside for a more romantic setting in lush gardens.

✉ Holetown, St James ☎ 432 8356, www.tidesbarbados.com ⦿ Lunch Mon–Fri, dinner Mon–Sun

SHOPPING

Cave Shepherd Sunset Crest Mall
A good selection of souvenirs, clothing, gifts, crafts, curios and rum, plus a decent bookshop.

✉ Sunset Crest Plaza No. 2, Holetown ⦿ Mon–Sat

Chalky Mount Potteries
Best places to see ➤ 42–43.

Earthworks Pottery
See pottery, from bowls to ornaments, being made and hand-decorated at this traditional pottery. Also clay, metalwork, glass and fabric designs (➤ 106).

✉ Edgehill, St Thomas ☎ 425 0223; www.earthworks-pottery.com ⦿ Mon–Fri 9–5, Sat 9–1

Gourmet Shop at Chattel Village
Edible treats, from Bajan hot sauce, nutmeg and vanilla beans to aged bourbons. Hand-rolled Cuban cigars also available.

✉ Chattel Village, Holetown ☎ 432 7711 ⦿ Mon–Sat 9–5:30

Old Pharmacy Art Gallery and Sculpture Terrace
Wide-ranging collection of paintings, sculpture and photographs by local artists in a beautifully restored townhouse. Artists' studios are situated out the back of the property. Across the road is a small seafront sculpture park with changing exhibits and a bar serving evening canapés and wine.

✉ Queen Street, Speightstown, St Peter ☎ 234 2494 ⦿ Mon–Sat 10–6

Shell Gallery
An outstanding collection of shells from around the world.

✉ Contentment, Gibbs, St Peter ☎ 422 2593 ⦿ Mon–Fri 9–5, Sat 9–2

ENTERTAINMENT

Fisherman's Pub and Beach Bar

The Sunset steel orchestra and floor show is on regularly, plus a Bajan buffet every Wednesday evening.

✉ Speightstown, St Peter ☎ 422 2703 ⏱ Open for drinks nightly

Lexies Piano Bar

Convivial bar with cabaret singer-owner and renowned guest pianists. Customers are encouraged to join in the sing-songs.

✉ Second Street, Holetown, St James ☎ 432 5399 ⏱ Daily 8:30pm–2am

One Love Rum Shop

The Sunday-night karaoke session is a Holetown institution: locals and visitors alike cram the street in front of the bar while participants belt out songs.

✉ First Street, Holetown ⏱ Hours erratic: most afternoons and evenings

Ragamuffins

This small friendly bar and restaurant gets packed on Sunday nights for the evening drag show. Booking essential.

✉ First Street, Holetown, St James ☎ 432 1295

SPORTS AND ACTIVITIES

ATV Tour

Three-hour, guided quad-bike tours in scenic routes, on and off road.

✉ Fitts Village, St James ☎ 432 1923 ⏱ Daily 10 and 2

Sandy Lane Country Club Golf Course

Open to all golfers on a pay-as-you-play basis. Stunning views of the west coast. Correct attire essential.

✉ St James ☎ 444 2500

Segway Tour

Off-the-beaten-track tours on Segways (a battery-powered scooter) in rugged cliff tops and pastures, led by enthusiastic guides. Booking essential.

✉ Cove Bay, St Lucy ☎ 426 5740 ⏱ Mon–Sat 9:30, 11:30 and 1:45

Southern Barbados

In the south of Barbados you will find the bustling capital, Bridgetown, and the airport, with attractions coming thick and fast between the two, all within easy reach of one another. Inland, however, forested terrain slopes upward to Gun Hill, from which there are amazing views right across the island.

Oistins

On the coast, dramatic cliffs rise up past South Point Lighthouse, sandy beaches and big rollers at their base, attracting surfers. The island's party scene is along the southwest coast at St Lawrence Gap, a fun-packed strip of bars, clubs, craft stalls, rum shacks and less expensive hotels, ideal for a family vacation.

BANKS (BARBADOS) BREWERIES

Wherever you go on the island you'll see black, red and white billboards announcing that, apart from rum, the only thing to drink on Barbados is Banks beer. During a tour of the brewery and "Brew-seum," just outside Bridgetown, you can see it being brewed, visit the old brew house and have a tasting. Notice that the copper kettles, used for the brewing process for 30 years, have been replaced by modern steel vats that can each hold 3,080gal (14,000L) of beer. Even more astounding is the bottling hall, where 250,000 bottles of Banks are capped each day.

➕ 2J ✉ St Michael ☎ 228 6486 🕐 Tours: Mon–Fri 10, 12 and 2
✋ Moderate 🍴 Bar for beer tasting, cafés and restaurants ($–$$$) in Bridgetown 🚌 From Bridgetown

BARBADOS CONCORDE EXPERIENCE

An attraction at Grantley Adams International Airport giving visitors a chance to find out all they ever wanted to know about Concorde, which used to fly regularly to the island. There's an interactive flight school, a departure lounge, an observation deck, and a multimedia interactive presentation projected along the entire length of the aircraft and including live sound effects of Concorde taking off and breaking the sound barrier. See the cockpit and a simulator, view historic photos of the aircraft and buy memorabilia in the gift shop.

www.barbadosconcorde.com

➕ 4K ✉ Grantley Adams International Airport, Christ Church ☎ 420 7738
🕐 Daily 9–6 ✋ Moderate 🍴 Café on site ($$)

THE CRANE

Try to visit this historic hotel on a Sunday morning so you can enjoy the brunch and foot-tapping live gospel by local singers. It takes place in the clifftop terrace restaurant overlooking the cliffs and the Atlantic. On one side is the hotel pool: the majestic white colonnades surrounding a circle of blue and backed by the ocean have been photographed by dozens of fashion magazines. On the other side, sheer cliffs drop to the pink sands of Crane Beach.

Opened in 1887 on the site of an 18th-century mansion and lit

by oil lamps, The Crane was the first resort hotel on Barbados. At that time, ladies bathed discreetly in a specially built area called "the horse." The original steps cut into the cliff, leading to "the horse," still remain. As for the name of the hotel, it came about when there was a small commercial port here and a crane was used to raise and lower cargo on and off the trading ships that docked.

➕ 5J ✉ Crane, St Philip ☎ 423 6220 ⏰ Brunch Sun 9:30am; singing Sun 10–11am; Bajan buffet Sun 12:30–3. Advance reservations essential 🍴 Restaurant ($$$) noted for its seafood, especially oysters (▷ 146) 🚌 From Bridgetown catch the Sam Lord bus

GUN HILL SIGNAL STATION

Even if you've already visited Grenade Hall Signal Station
(► 112) and learned about the signal stations' important role in
the early communications network of Barbados, Gun Hill Signal
Station is still worth a visit for the views. It was built in 1818 and
was reputedly the cream of the string of stations established to
warn of slave uprisings. Eventually they served as lookouts for
cargo ships. Restored by the Barbados National Trust, Gun Hill,
perched on a ridge overlooking the St George Valley and the
south of the island, features a gray flag tower and a small
collection of memorabilia. For travelers with time it's a quiet
place to while away a few hours or wait for the best views,
which occur around sunset. The clear air was considered
particularly healthy and during the 19th century sick soldiers
came here to convalesce. Note the British Military Lion, a white
figure carved from limestone in the 19th century by the adjutant-
general of the Imperial Forces, who was stationed on the island.
A plaque below the lion states his name and reads that the

British lion shall "…rule from the rivers to the sea and from the sea to the ends of the earth."

✚ 3H ✉ St George ☎ 429 1358 🕐 Mon–Sat 9–5 🍴 Café ($); opening hours restricted 🚌 From Bridgetown take the Sergeant Street bus

HERITAGE PARK AND FOURSQUARE RUM DISTILLERY

Voted by an American newspaper as "one of the most modern rum distilleries in the world," the Heritage Park and Foursquare Rum Distillery was the project of Barbadian businessman and rum producer David Seale. The distillery has its own integrated recycling plant. If that alone isn't a sufficient draw, there's more to see at this attraction, which covers 7 acres (3ha) of a once sprawling sugar plantation and includes one of the island's oldest sugar factories. In an outdoor museum filled with machinery, you can see how rum was made in the early days, or you can go underground to the furnace and feel what it was like to be a boiler worker. Nowadays, the distillery is known for its top-selling ESAF White Rum, Orland Brigand and Doorly's Rum, which you are given the opportunity to taste. Capitalizing on the popularity of the Heritage Park, there are exhibitions of paintings by local artists in the on-site art galleries.

✚ 5J ✉ Foursquare, St Philip ☎ 420 9954 🕐 Mon–Fri 9–5 ✋ Moderate 🚌 From Bridgetown take the St Patrick bus

OISTINS

By day, Oistins is a busy fishing village that supplies fresh fish and shellfish to the whole of the island. Boats are forever landing catches or are pulled up on the grassy sand dunes for repair or paintwork. Walk among the lobster pots and nets, then watch the fishmongers gutting and packing the fish in ice at the fish terminal. You can get a cheap bite to eat here at lunchtime, but the real draw is the enormously popular Friday-night Fish Fry, when stallholders fry flying fish, dolphin, shark, barracuda and snapper.

Order your fish with rice or a helping of macaroni cheese pie and a bottle of Banks beer. There's music, long lines at the counters and dancing by the tables. Saturday nights are also popular, but even better is the Oistins Fish Festival, which runs over Easter.

➕ 3K ✉ Christ Church 🍴 Excellent freshly fried fish at stalls ($)
🚌 From Bridgetown

ORCHID WORLD

Best places to see ➤ 44–45.

RAGGED POINT

An old lighthouse marks Ragged Point, the most easterly point of the island. It is a wonderfully exposed, tranquil spot. Though the lighthouse is no longer open to the public, its beams still warn ships away from the limestone cliffs and Cobbler's Reef. Slightly to the north of the lighthouse is tiny, uninhabited Culpepper Island, Barbados's only "colony".

➕ 6H ✉ St Philip 🍴 Cafés and restaurants ($–$$$) en route 🚌 To Crane Beach or Sam Lord's Castle ♿ Free

ST GEORGE VALLEY

St George Valley is an agricultural oasis covered with sugar-cane fields. St George Parish Church stands proudly as one of only four churches on the island to survive the hurricane of 1831. Built in 1784, the church boasts a splendid altar painting called *Rise to Power*. It is the work of artist Benjamin West, the first American president of the Royal Academy. Richard Westmacott, the sculptor of the statue of Lord Nelson in Bridgetown, also created some sculptures here inside the church.

➕ 3H

a drive and Sunday brunch

One Sunday morning, having reserved tickets in advance, skip breakfast and head along the south coast to hear gospel singing at The Crane hotel (▶ 133). En route you'll see Bajan women in dresses, hats and white gloves attending church. Some men wear their Sunday best suits. Quietly and unobtrusively, stop outside any church and listen to the hymns.

Start from Oistins (▶ 136) on the Maxwell main road and head east, following the signs to the airport. You'll drive through villages with painted houses and cane fields. Follow the signs to Crane Beach.

Arrive at The Crane hotel at 9:30am in time for Sunday brunch while you enjoy the entertainment (advance reservations are essential). Afterward, walk down to Crane Bay for some swimming, sunbathing or bodyboarding.

Drive out of Crane Beach and head north, finishing up at Ragged Point (▶ 137) for a brief walk and lunch (if you're still hungry).

On the drive back you can take a right detour to Sunbury Plantation House (▶ 54) for afternoon tea before heading back towards Oistins.

If the day is still young, take a left detour through small communities to reach Silver Sands beach (▶ 141).

Watch the windsurfers flip 360 degrees above the waves. Look for the South Point Lighthouse, made in England out of cast iron and shipped in pieces to the island. It was reassembled and working by 1852.

Alternatively, head straight back along the coastal road to Oistins fishing village for the perfect finale – a succulent fish fry in the open air at one of the many shacks.

Distance Approx 7 miles (12km) **Time** Half a day with brunch and stops
Start Point Oistins ✚ 3K **End Point** Ragged Point ✚ 6H
Brunch The Crane hotel ($$$) (➤ 133, 146)

ST LAWRENCE GAP

Moving westward along the south coast, the closer you get to
Bridgetown the livelier it becomes. St Lawrence Gap is where the
party people go, although regulars say it's not as friendly and easy-
going as it used to be. Sports bars with video screens, live blues,
happy hours and karaoke, souvenir shells and painted maracas are
what it's all about. There's a string of good restaurants and, in
between the hotels and apartment buildings, crescents of sandy
beach and safe swimming. You can learn to dive, water-ski or just
hang onto a banana boat.

🚻 2K 🖂 South coast, east of Bridgetown 🍽 Bars and restaurants ($–$$),
some with live music 🚌 Any south coast bus from Bridgetown

SILVER SANDS

Silver Sands beach, at the southern tip of the island, is a magnet for professional windsurfers, and there's a Club Mistral center here for lessons and equipment rental. In addition to windsurfing you can try boogie boarding, hiking and wilderness and adventure diving. As the beach's name suggests, less adventurous types can relax on the beautiful silver sands and watch others hard at play.

✚ 4L ✉ Silver Sands, Christ Church
🍴 Snacks ($) nearby

SUNBURY PLANTATION HOUSE

Best places to see ➤ 54–55.

WILDEY HOUSE

Wildey House, a Georgian hilltop mansion set in beautiful grounds, is the headquarters of the Barbados National Trust. Although the building is not in the best state of repair, visitors will see historic photographs of Barbados and exquisite silver displayed among antique furniture in carefully decorated rooms. The Trust is important to the island because it enables its architecture,

sometimes dating back more than 350 years, to be preserved and maintained. Since 1961 the Trust has taken on the care of eight properties, including a wooded gully (➤ 121), the largest sugar mill in the Caribbean (➤ 116) and a botanic garden (➤ 36). It has also helped to create an underwater park (➤ 110) on the west coast and has identified Bush Hill (➤ 47, 92) as the house in which George Washington, president of the United States, stayed in 1751.

➕ 2J ✉ Wildey, St Michael ☎ 426 2421 ⊘ By appointment

an excursion

A submarine cruise

There are few places in the world where you can board a real submarine and submerge for an undersea exploration. Complete with Captain Nemo-style sounds and live dialogue between the crew and the surface, the Atlantis Submarine trip is pricey, but shouldn't be missed.

First, you board the *Ocean Crest* catamaran and sail out of Bridgetown's harbor to reach the submarine. Safety instructions are given before you are invited to board.

In 1994 *Atlantis* became the world's first passenger submarine. Stretching 66ft (20m) and displacing 80 tons, the *Atlantis III* sinks slowly to 151ft (46m). It then cruises gently above the seabed off the west coast at 1.5 knots. You sit with the other passengers on benches, facing outward, looking through large portholes.

The seabed is white, like fallen snow. A wreck appears, the fish darting in and out of its gaps. Next comes a garden of brain coral, ferns and sponges. If you're lucky, a turtle might glide gracefully by. You'll definitely see thousands of fish, from stingrays to barracudas and shoals of colorful species. If you've ever wanted to scuba dive but lacked the courage, this is the next best thing.

Even more spectacular is Atlantis By Night, a cruise taken when the coral is at its most striking and nocturnal predators come out to feed. The submarine's lights

illuminate the coral and fish and you'll see the wreck of the *Lord Willoughby*. Whichever trip you take, at the end you're given a certificate to prove that you took the plunge.

Time 1 hour
Start/End point Atlantis Submarines ✉ Shallow Draught, Bridgetown ☎ 436 8968; www.atlantisadventures.com
🖐 Expensive 🚌 Nearest bus station is Bridgetown; take a taxi to the harbor ❓ Book through Atlantis Submarines, a tour operator, or your hotel or resort rep

HOTELS

▼▼▼ Accra Beach Hotel and Resort ($–$$)

An elegant and longstanding hotel set on a spectacular beach of soft white sands, with an attractive new spa offering all kinds of treatments. Frequent live entertainment for guests includes a Thursday barbecue and floor show with stiltwalking, calypso and limbo dancing, steel pan music at lunchtime on Sundays and karaoke nights.

✉ Christ Church ☎ 435 8920; www.accrabeachhotel.com

▼▼▼ Bougainvillea Beach Resort ($$–$$$)

Overlooking the Caribbean, this luxury resort features suites with kitchen facilities. There is a choice of restaurants, a kids' club, pool, water sports and tennis facilities.

✉ Christ Church ☎ 418 0990; www.bougainvillearesort.com

▼▼▼ ▼▼▼ The Crane ($$$)

This 18th-century hotel is most noted for its fabulous location perched on a cliff overlooking the pink sands of Crane Bay, one of the island's most famous and beautiful beaches (▶ 133). There are several restaurants on the property; particularly noteworthy is Zen, which has the best Japanese food on the island. New development includes an attractive shopping village with boutiques and gift shops.

✉ St Philip ☎ 423 6220; www.thecrane.com

▼▼▼ Little Arches ($$$)

Luxury adults-only boutique hotel close to the fishing village of Oistins. Secluded and private, with an excellent restaurant on site, Café Luna, and overlooking lovely Enterprise Beach. Ten rooms are decorated with stylish Mediterranean features; some have kitchen facilities and plunge pools.

✉ Enterprise Beach Road, Christ Church ☎ 420 4689; www.littlearches.com

▼▼▼ Sea Breeze Resort ($$)

Recently renovated, this all-inclusive hotel has comfortable rooms, two pools and several attractive dining options. Additional features include full water-sports facilities and beach-bar service on one of the south coast's prettiest stretches of sand.

✉ Maxwell Beach Road, Christ Church ☎ 420 4689; www.sea-breeze.com

♦♦♦ Turtle Beach ($$)

An attractive all-inclusive resort, which is one of the island's most popular hotels and is the host for numerous weddings. The excellent amenities include two swimming pools, a breezy open-air eating area, comprehensive water sports and a particularly lovely and large stretch of beach. Staff are extremely attentive and there is an excellent Italian restaurant as well as the usual buffet dining.

✉ St Lawrence Gap ☎ 428 7131; www.turtlebeachresortbarbados.com

RESTAURANTS

♦♦♦ Apsara/Tamnak Thai ($$$)

Twin restaurants, Indian and Thai, in a joint venture in an old plantation house with lush tropical gardens and a serene atmosphere. Authentic and imaginative dishes prepared by specialists in both cuisines.

✉ Morecambe House, Worthing, Christ Church ☎ 435 5454/5446; www.apsarabarbados.com 🕐 Mon–Fri lunch, Mon–Sun dinner

♦♦♦ Bellinis ($$–$$$)

This cosy little trattoria on the waterfront offers a wide range of Italian dishes, among them are gourmet pizzas and fresh pasta made in-house daily. The ubiquitous Bellini cocktail served here is delicious and should not be missed.

✉ Little Bay Hotel, St Lawrence Gap, Christ Church ☎ 420 7587; www.bellinisbarbados.com 🕐 Daily dinner only

♦♦ Bistro Monet ($$)

Traditional French food and modern international cuisine are served up in this popular little bistro at very reasonable prices. Friendly and casual atmosphere.

✉ Hastings Main Road, Christ Church ☎ 435 9389 🕐 Mon–Fri 11–10, Sat 6–10

✿✿ Black Pearl ($$$)

Seafood and steakhouse with two bars specializing in cocktails and good wine. Owner Dimitri Vamvakas brings a touch of Greece to the dishes.

✉ Shak Shak Complex, Hastings, Christ Church ☎ 435 1234; www.blackpearlbarbados.com 🕐 Mon–Fri lunch, daily dinner

✿ Bubba's Sports Bar and Restaurant ($)

Air-conditioned eatery serving local and international cuisine with satellite screens showing major sporting events.

✉ Rodeley Main Road, Christ Church ☎ 435 8731; www.bubbassportsbar.net 🕐 Daily lunch and dinner

✿ Café Sol Mexican Grill and Margarita Bar ($)

A crowded yet fashionable haunt, specializing in big plates of nachos, salads and the typical Mexican fare, plus a gringo menu for the less adventurous. Drinks include tall cocktails and there are occasional deals such as two-for-one drinks. The last Friday of the month plays host to a riotous party with half-price Tequila shots and Margaritas.

✉ St Lawrence Gap, Christ Church ☎ 420 7655; www.cafesolbarbados.com 🕐 Tue–Sun lunch, daily dinner

✿✿ David's Place by the Sea ($$)

Traditional Bajan fare, cooked to a very high standard, including spicy pepperpot soup and excellent flying fish. Portions are generous and the longstanding staff are known for their warmth and friendliness.

✉ St Lawrence Gap, Christ Church ☎ 435 9755; www.davidsplacebarbados 🕐 Tue–Sun dinner only

✿✿ Flying Fish Restaurant and Bar ($–$$)

A bistro within the Yellow Bird Hotel overlooking St Lawrence Bay. Award-winning cuisine includes flying fish prepared eight ways, as well as traditional English fare and Lobster Night on Saturdays.

✉ St Lawrence Gap, Christ Church ☎ 418 9772; www.yellowbirdhotel.com 🕐 Daily breakfast, lunch and dinner

Fusion ($$)

Stylish and fashionable open-air bar with lounging areas and extensive cocktail menu. The indoors restaurant serves Thai and Japanese dishes, specializing in sushi.

✉ South Beach Hotel, Rockley, Christ Church ☎ 436 1538 🕐 Tue–Sat lunch, Tue–Sun dinner

💎💎 Harlequin ($$)

An intimate restaurant with a friendly British owner who creates a warm atmosphere. The standard international fare offers an eclectic range of dishes, including a long vegetarian menu and fresh local fish. Cocktails are excellent and children are made particularly welcome.

✉ St Lawrence Gap ☎ 420 7677; www.harlequinrestaurant.com 🕐 Daily dinner only

💎💎💎 Josef's ($$$)

Extravagant seafood dishes and wines from around the world are served in this very classy signature restaurant by the beach. Kampai Japanese Restaurant upstairs.

✉ St Lawrence Gap, Christ Church ☎ 420 7638; www.josefsinbarbados.com 🕐 Daily dinner only

💎 Lucky Horseshoe ($–$$)

Open 24 hours for steaks, omelettes and waffles, a "trail blazing" BBQ buffet, spare ribs, pasta, rice and potatoes. Good kids' menu.

✉ Worthing Main Road, Christ Church ☎ 435 5825; www.luckyh.com 🕐 24 hours

Oistins Fish Market ($)

Amazing Fish Fry on Friday evenings, when diners dance among the tables. At stalls and huts, freshly caught flying fish, dolphin, snapper, barbecued pig and chicken are cooked to take away or you can eat at the handy benches and tables (► 136).

✉ Oistins village, Christ Church 🕐 Mostly at night, some stalls are open throughout the day

Steak House Barbados ($–$$)

US sizzling steaks are served on signature cast-iron "cows," and there's also a salad bar, pasta, seafood, chicken and lamb. On the same site, St Lawrence Pizza Hut offers pizzas and hamburgers.

✉ St Lawrence Gap, Christ Church ☎ 428 7152; www.steakhousebarbados.com 🕐 Daily 9am–11pm

☗ Sweet Potatoes ($–$$)

Friendly, clean and well-priced restaurant with Bajan specialties and cocktails. Karaoke on Mondays and live steel pan music on Wednesdays.

✉ St Lawrence Gap, Christ Church ☎ 420 7668; www.thegapbarbados.com/sweetpotatoes 🕐 Daily

Tapas ($$)

Tapas restaurant in a pretty spot on the beach and the new south coast boardwalk. As well as tapas, hungry customers can choose from main menu dishes; these have an Italian influence.

✉ Main Road, Hastings, Christ Church ☎ 228 0704 🕐 Daily 5pm–11pm

☗☗☗ Zen ($$–$$$)

Spectacular setting high above Crane Beach with an all-glass frontage. Superb award-winning Japanese cuisine with a sushi bar and separate tatami room.

✉ The Crane Resort, Crane, St Philip ☎ 423 6220; www.thecrane.com 🕐 Wed–Mon dinner only

SHOPPING

Chattel House Shopping Village

Colorful chattel-style houses turned into crammed boutique shops. Souvenirs, beachwear, T-shirts and jewelry.

✉ St Lawrence Gap, Christ Church ☎ 428 2472 🕐 Mon–Sat 9–6

Lazy Dayz Surf Shop

All kinds of beachwear, with a wide range of bikinis, shorts, T-shirts, sarongs and beach accessories.

✉ Quayside Centre, Rockley, Christ Church ☎ 435 8115 🕐 Mon–Sat 9–6

Rockley Beach Seaside Shopping

Half a dozen kiosks in the park behind the beach sell all kinds of souvenirs, crafts and colorful summer clothing.

✉ Rockley Beach, Christ Church 🕐 Mon–Sat 9–6

Sheraton Centre

Barbados's first and largest shopping mall, with 120 units selling accessories, clothes, shoes, souvenirs, electrical goods and books. Also home to a multiplex cinema, one of only a few on the island.

✉ Sargeants Village, Christ Church ☎ 437 0970 🕐 Mon–Sat 9–9

ENTERTAINMENT

St Lawrence Gap, Christ Church, is the throbbing heart of Barbados, with clubs, bars and restaurants open until late. Happy hours are usually hosted early evening. It is best to arrive at a nightclub well after 10pm. Local live bands are highly talented.

39 Steps Wine Bar

Relaxing wine bar with live jazz every other Saturday night and guitar music every other Friday.

✉ Chattel Plaza, Hastings, Christ Church ☎ 427 0715 🕐 Mon–Fri noon–midnight, Sat 6pm–midnight

Bajan Roots and Rhythms

A Caribbean show, carnival, extravaganza and dinner-party buffet with unlimited drinks. This is one of the island's most popular attractions, so booking in advance is essential.

✉ Plantation Theatre, St Lawrence ☎ 428 5048; www.plantationtheatre.com 🕐 Wed and Fri from 7pm

Bert's Bar

Catch up with sports and world news live on satellite television. Popular slot machines and a famous daiquiri drink. Plus you can munch on stone-fired pizzas.

✉ Rockley, Christ Church ☎ 435 7924; www.bertsbarbados.com 🕐 Daily until 1am, happy hour Mon–Fri 4:30pm–6pm

Bubba's Sports Bar and Restaurant

Live sporting action is shown on three huge screens and on additional TVs.

✉ Rodeley Main Road, Christ Church ☎ 435 8731; www.bubbassportsbar.net 🕓 Mon–Sat 10–midnight, Sun 9–midday

The Crane

Visit the clifftop terrace restaurant at this historic hotel on a Sunday morning to enjoy the amazing gospel singing and brunch (➤ 133) that's become an island institution. Advance reservations are essential.

✉ St Philip ☎ 423 6220; www.thecrane.com 🕓 Sun 9:30–noon

Lucky Horseshoe

A 24-hour joint for gamblers with slot machines and large screens showing sport and music via satellite. American fast food round the clock.

✉ Worthing Main Road, Christ Church ☎ 435 5825; www.luckyh.com 🕓 24 hours

McBridges Pub and Cookhouse

Live music and dancing every night in a popular Irish pub with an extended happy hour between 11pm and 1am. Food is also available in the form of pizzas, burgers, ribs and British/Irish-style pub meals.

✉ St Lawrence Gap ☎ 435 6352; www.mcbridesbarbados.com 🕓 Daily; music 10pm–late

Reggae Lounge

Reggae, calypso and other Caribbean hits played by the island's DJs to a packed dance floor in the open air. Regular live bands.

✉ St Lawrence Gap ☎ 435 6462 🕓 Nightly

Ship Inn

This long-established nightspot, with different live music acts and DJs every night, is a good choice for either a meal or a night out. Soul Stew on Mondays and a Back in Time party on Fridays are particularly popular. There are two restaurants on this site and late-night snacks are available until the wee hours.

✉ St Lawrence Gap ☎ 420 7447; www.shipinnbarbados.com ⏰ Daily 10:30pm–late

Whistling Frog

Solid street pub with occasional live music and DJ.

✉ St Lawrence Gap ☎ 420 5021 ⏰ 24 hours

SPORTS AND ACTIVITIES

Barbados Golf Club

In the south of Durrants, close to the airport. Par 72, pay-as-you-play course redesigned in 2000. It has since hosted the Barbados open twice.

✉ Durrants, Christ Church ☎ 428 8463; www.barbadosgolfclub.com

DeAction Beach

Brian 'Irie Man' Talma is Barbados's best windsurfer and at Silver Sands, one of the most blustery points on the island, he rents out equipment and gives lessons to beginners. Kite-surfing and surfing enthusiasts are also catered for.

✉ Silver Sands, Christ Church ☎ 428 6596; www.briantalma.com

Island Safari

Exciting adventure tours with knowledgable local guides.

✉ Bush Hall Main Road, St Michael ☎ 429 5337; www.islandsafari.bb

Rockley Golf and Country Club

Rockley is the oldest club on the island and has a pleasant 9-hole course offering pay and play.

✉ Rockley, Christ Church ☎ 435 7873; www.rockleygolfcourse.com

Surf Barbados

Surf tours, lessons and rentals for adults and children over eight to suit a range of abilities. A maximum tutorial group of four people per instructor allows for more personal lessons.

✉ Varies according to surf conditions ☎ 256 3906; www.surfing-barbados.com

Index

ABC Highway 70–71
Accra Beach 60
Adams, Sir Grantley 94
adventure safaris 27, 72, 153
Aerial Trek 62, 100
air travel 25, 26
All Saints Church 118
Almond Beach Village 123
Andromeda Botanic Gardens 19, 36–37
Animal Flower Cave 101
Arbib Nature & Heritage Trail 122–123
Arlington House 52, 102
Arnold, William 118
Atlantis Submarine 19, 62, 144–145

banks 29, 31
Banks (Barbados) Breweries 132
baobab tree 88
Barbados Concorde Experience 132
Barbados Museum and Historical Society 76, 91
Barbados National Trust 72, 77, 142–143
Barbados Polo Club 103
Barbados Wildlife Reserve 38–39, 62
Barclays Park 104
Barrow, Errol Walton 51
Bathsheba 16, 40–41, 60
beaches 60–61
beer brewery tour 132
Belleplaine 105
boat trips and cruises 18, 26, 62, 72, 98, 110, 144–145
bodyboarding 60, 72
Bottom Bay 60
Bridgetown 16, 81–98
  Barbados Museum and Historical Society 76, 91
  Bridgetown Synagogue 82
  Careenage 83
  entertainment 98
  Garrison Historic Area 46–47
  George Washington House 47, 92
  hotels 96
  Montefiore Fountain 84
  Mount Gay Rum Visitor Centre 92–93

National Heroes Square 50–51
Parliament Buildings 84–85
Pelican Craft Centre 93
Queen's Park 86, 88
restaurants 96–97
St Michael's Cathedral 89
St Patrick's Cathedral 94
shoping 97–98
sights 82–95
sport and activities 98
Tyrol Cot Heritage Village 94–95
walk 86–87
British Military Lion 134–135
buses 26, 27
Bussa 70

car rental 28
Careenage 83
catamaran cruises 72, 98
Cattlewash 40
cave systems
  Animal Flower Cave 101
  Harrison's Cave 48–49, 62
Chalky Mount Potteries 42–43
Charles Fort 46
chattel houses 70, 104, 123
children's entertainment 62
cinema 77
climate and seasons 22
coconut palms 65
concessions 27
The Crane 133, 138
Crane Bay 61, 138
credit cards 29
cricket 11, 47, 72, 98
crime 31
Crop Over 24
cruise ships 25
Culpepper Island 137
cultural activities 76–77

diving 16, 19, 23, 66–67, 110
Dottins Reef 66, 110
Dover Fort 123
drinking water 31
drives
  ABC Highway 70–71
  East Coast Road 104–105
  northern Barbados 118–119
  southern Barbados 138–139
driving 22, 28
drugs and medicines 31

Earthworks Pottery 106, 129
East Coast Road 104–105
electricity 31
Emancipation Statue 70, 71
embassies and consulates 30
entertainment
  Bridgetown 98
  northern Barbados 130
  southern Barbados 151–153
excursions 27

Fairmont Royal Pavilion Estate 108
Farley Hill National Park 107
festivals and events 24
fishing 72
Fitts Village 61
Flower Forest 44, 45
Folkestone Marine Reserve 110
food and drink 12–15
  alcoholic drinks 14–15
  Bajan sauce 12–13
  drinking water 31
  national dishes 12–14
  non-alcoholic drinks 15
  rum 14, 18, 92–93, 135
  snacks 15
  see also restaurants
four-wheel drive tours 27, 72
Foursquare Rum Distillery 135
Frank Hutson Sugar Museum 111

gardens
  Andromeda Botanic Gardens 19, 36–37
  Fairmont Royal Pavilion Estate 108
  Flower Forest 44, 45
  Hunte's Gardens 115
  Orchid World 44–45
Garrison Historic Area 46–47
George Washington House 47, 92
glass-bottomed boat tours 110
golf 72, 130, 153
gospel music 17, 24, 138
Government House 71
Grenade Hall Forest and Signal Station 112–113
Gun Hill Signal Station 134–135

Harbour Master Cruises 62
Harrison's Cave 18, 48–49, 62
health 22, 23, 30–31
Heritage Park 135
hiking 27
historic houses
  Arlington House 52, 102
  chattel houses 70, 104, 123
  Farley Hill National Park 107
  George Washington House
    47, 92
  St Nicholas Abbey 116–117
  Sunbury Plantation House
    54–55
  Tyrol Cot Heritage Village
    94–95
  Wildey House 142–143
Holetown 113–114
horse racing 24, 47, 72
horseback riding 72
hotels 74–75
  Bridgetown 96
  Northern Barbados 124–126
  southern Barbados 146–147
Hunte's Gardens 115

Independence Arch 83
inoculations 22
insurance 22, 23
internet services 29

Jewish Synagogue 82

language 32

medical treatment 23
money 29
Montefiore Fountain 84
Morgan Lewis Sugar Mill 116
Mount Gay Rum Visitor Centre
  92–93
Mount Hillaby 44
Mullins Bay 61, 64–65
museum opening hours 31

National Heroes Gallery 85
National Heroes Square 50–51
national holidays 23
nightlife see entertainment
North Point 101, 119
northern Barbados 99–130
  drive 118–119
  entertainment 130
  hotels 124–126
  restaurants 126–129

shopping 129
sights 100–123
sports and activities 130

Oistins 17, 136–137
opening hours 31
Orchid World 44–45

Parliament Buildings 84–85
passports and visas 22
Paynes Bay 61
Pelican Craft Centre 93
personal safety 31
pharmacies 31
polo 103
Port St Charles 123
postal services 29, 31
pottery 42–43, 106
Prescod, Samuel Jackman 51
public transport 26

quad-bike tours 130
Queen's Park 86, 88
Queen's Park House 88

radio 77
Ragged Point 137
restaurants 58–59
  Barbados Gourmet Card 27
  Bridgetown 96–97
  northern Barbados 126–129
  southern Barbados 147–150
rum 14, 18, 92–93, 135

St George Parish Church 137
St George Valley 137
St Lawrence Gap 71, 140
St Michael's Cathedral 89
St Nicholas Abbey 116–117
St Patrick's Cathedral 94
St Peter's Parish Church 53
Sandy Beach 61
Scotland District 43, 104
Segways tours 130
shopping
  Bridgetown 97–98
  northern Barbados 129
  opening hours 31
  southern Barbados 150–151
Silver Sands 61, 138–139, 141
Six Men's Bay 117
South Point Lighthouse 139
southern Barbados 131–153
  drive 138–139
  entertainment 151–153

hotels 146–147
restaurants 147–150
shopping 150–151
sights 132–145
sports and activities 153
Speightstown 52–53
sports and activities 72
  Bridgetown 98
  northern Barbados 130
  southern Barbados 153
Springvale Eco-Heritage
  Museum 76, 120
submarine cruise 144–145
sugar industry 111, 116
sun safety 30–31
Sunbury Plantation House
  54–55

taxis 28
telephones 30
time differences 23
tipping 29
tourist information 22–23, 29
turtles 64–65, 72
Tyrol Cot Heritage Village
  94–95

views 68–69

walks
  Arbib Nature and Heritage
    Trail 122–123
  Bridgetown 86–87
  Mullins Bay 64–65
Washington, George 92
websites 22
Welchman Hall Gully 121
West, Benjamin 137
Westmacott, Richard 137
Wildey House 142–143
wildlife reserve 38–39, 62
windsurfing 60, 61, 139, 141,
  153
wreck diving 67

Acknowledgements

The Automobile Association wishes to thank the following photographers for their assistance in the preparation of this book.

Abbreviations for the picture credits are as follows – (t) top; (b) bottom; (l) left; (r) right; (c) centre; (AA) AA World Travel Library

4l Mullins Bay, AA/J Tims; **4c** Heroes Square, Bridgetown, AA/J Tims; **4r** Rock formations, Bathsheba, AA/J Tims; **5l** Fairmont Royal Pavilion Hotel, AA/J Tims; **5c** Boardwalk, St Lawrence, AA/J Tims; **6/7** Mullins Bay, AA/J Tims; **8/9** Souvenirs, Bathsheba, AA/J Tims; **10/11t** Palm trees, Bottom Bay, AA/J Tims; **10cr** Souvenirs, Bathsheba, AA/J Tims; **10bl** Andromeda Botanic Gardens, AA/J Tims; **10br** Oistin's Friday night Fish Fry, AA/J Tims; **11cl** Shop, Speightstown, AA/J Tims; **11bl** Race Day, Garrison Savannah, AA/J Tims; **11br** Handbags, Holetown festival, AA/J Tims; **12/13t** Filleting flying fish, Six Men's Bay, AA/J Tims; **12bl** Hot Sauce on sale, AA/J Tims; **12br** Detail of breadfruit, AA/J Tims; **13tr** Bajan bread, AA/J Tims; **13cr** Green bananas, AA/J Tims; **14tl** Oistin's Friday night Fish Fry, AA/J Tims; **14bl** Mount Gay Rum, AA/J Tims; **14br** Advertising, Banks Brewery, AA/J Tims; **15tl** Cocktails, AA/J Tims; **15cl** Coconut ready to drink, Bottom Bay, AA/J Tims; **15cr** Round House Bar, Cattlewash, AA/J Tims; **16/17t** Souvenir stalls, Bridgetown, AA/J Tims; **16c** Turtle, Oistins, AA/J Tims; **16b** Coastline, Bathsheba, AA/J Tims; **17tr** Statue, Crane Beach, AA/J Tims; **17b** Oistin's Friday night Fish Fry, AA/J Tims; **18/19t** Sunset, Paynes Bay, AA/J Tims; **18/19b** Foursquare Rum Distillery & Heritage Park, AA/J Tims; **19br** Andromeda Botanic Gardens, AA/J Tims; **20/21** Heroes Square, Bridgetown, AA/J Tims; **24** The Holetown Dooflicky festival, AA/J Tims; **25** Cruise ship, AA/D Lyons; **26** Bus, Bathsheba, AA/J Tims; **27** Island Safari Jeep Tours, AA/J Tims; **28** Taxi, AA/J Tims; **29** Telephone box, AA/J Tims; **30** Policeman, AA/J Tims; **32** Pavement market stall, Speightstown, AA/J Tims; **34/35** Rock formation, Bathsheba, AA/J Tims; **36cl** Andromeda Botanic Gardens, AA/J Tims; **36cb** Hibiscus Café, Andromeda Botanic Gardens, AA/J Tims; **36/37c** Andromeda Botanic Gardens, AA/J Tims; **37tr** Talipot Palm trees, Corypha umbraculifera, Andromeda Botanic Gardens, AA/J Tims; **38c** Barbados Green or Vervet monkey, AA/J Tims; **38bl** Two iguanas, Barbados Wildlife Reserve, AA/J Tims; **39t** Mahogany bar area, Barbados Wildlife Reserve, AA/J Tims; **39c** Goose, Barbados Wildlife Reserve, AA/J Tims; **40c** Surfing, Bathsheba, AA/J Tims; **40/41b** East Coast near Cattlewash, AA/J Tims; **41t** Shop, Bathsheba, AA/J Tims; **42** Highland Pottery, Chalky Mount Village, AA/J Tims; **43t** View from the Highland Pottery, Chalky Mount Village, AA/J Tims; **43cr** Vase, Highland Pottery, Chalky Mount Village, AA/J Tims; **43br** Bar, Chalky Mount Village, AA/J Tims; **44l** Red Ginger Flower, Alpinia purpurata, Flower Forest, AA/J Tims; **44/45c** Tropical corridor of palms, Flower Forest, AA/J Tims; **45r** Flower Forest, AA/J Tims; **46l** Garrison Historic Area, AA/J Tims; **46/47c** St Ann's Fort, Garrison Historic Area, AA/J Tims; **47t** Race Day, Garrison Savannah, AA/J Tims; **48/49** Harrison's Cave, Tony Arruza/CORBIS; **50b** Fountain, National Heroes Square, Bridgetown, AA/J Tims; **51tr** Nelson's Monument, National Heroes Square, Bridgetown, AA/J Tims; **51cr** War Memorial, Heroes Square, Bridgetown, AA/J Tims; **52b** Pier, Speightstown, AA/J Tims; **52/53t** Speightstown, AA/J Tims; **53c** St Peter's Parish Church, Speightstown, AA/J Tims; **54** Prints of paintings by Augustino Brunias (1771), Sunbury Plantation House, AA/J Tims; **54cl** Study, Sunbury Plantation House, AA/J Tims; **55t** Bath, Sunbury Plantation House, AA/J Tims; **55b** Sunbury Plantation House, AA/J Tims; **56/57** Outdoor dinning area, Fairmont Royal Pavilion Hotel, AA/J Tims; **58/59** Round House Bar, Cattlewash, AA/J Tims; **60/61** Accra or Rockley beach, AA/J Tims; **63** Barbados Wildlife Reserve, AA/J Tims; **64** Cobblers Cove, AA/J Tims; **65tr** Mullins Bay, AA/J Tims; **66/67b** Dive boat, Bridgetown, AA/J Tims; **67tr** Air tanks, AA/J Tims; **68/69** Bathsheba, AA/J Tims;

Sight locator index

This index relates to the maps on the covers. We have given map references to the main sights of interest in the book. Grid references in italics indicate sights featured on town plans. Some sights within towns may not be plotted on the maps.

Andromeda Botanic Gardens **4F**

Animal Flower Cave **2C**

Banks Breweries **2J**

Barbados Concorde Experience **4K**

Barbados Museum and Historical Society **2K**

Barbados Polo Club **1H**

Barbados Wildlife Reserve **2E**

Bathsheba **4F**

Bridgetown **2J**

Bridgetown Synagogue ***Bridgetown 4c***

The Careenage ***Bridgetown 3e***

Chalky Mount Village **3F**

The Crane **5J**

Earthworks Pottery **2G**

Fairmont Royal Pavilion **1F**

Farley Hill National Park **2E**

Flower Forest **3F**

Folkestone Marine Reserve **1G**

Foursquare Rum Distillery **5J**

Frank Hutson Sugar Museum **2G**

Garrison Historic Area **2K**

Graeme Hall Bird Sanctuary **2K**

Grenade Hall Forest and Signal Station **2E**

Gun Hill Signal Station **3H**

Harrison's Cave **3G**

Holetown **1G**

Montefiore Fountain ***Bridgetown 4b***

Morgan Lewis Sugar Mill **2D**

Mount Gay Rum Visitor Centre **1J**

National Heroes Square ***Bridgetown 5d***

Ocean Park Aquarium **4K**

Oistins **3K**

Orchid World **3H**

Parliament Buildings ***Bridgetown 5d***

Pelican Craft Centre **1J**

Queen's Park ***Bridgetown 8c***

Ragged Point **6H**

St George Valley **3H**

St Lawrence Gap **2K**

St Michael's Cathedral ***Bridgetown 6d***

St Nicholas Abbey **2D**

St Patrick's Cathedral **2J**

Silver Sands **4L**

Six Men's Bay **1E**

Speightstown **1E**

Sunbury Plantation House **4J**

Tryol Cot Heritage Village **2J**

Welchman Gully **2G**

Wildey House **2J**

Dear Reader

Your comments, opinions and recommendations are very important to us. Please help us to improve our travel guides by taking a few minutes to complete this simple questionnaire.

You do not need a stamp (unless posted outside the UK). If you do not want to cut this page from your guide, then photocopy it or write your answers on a plain sheet of paper.

Send to: **The Editor, AA World Travel Guides,
FREEPOST SCE 4598, Basingstoke RG21 4GY.**

Your recommendations...

We always encourage readers' recommendations for restaurants, nightlife or shopping – if your recommendation is used in the next edition of the guide, we will send you a **FREE AA Guide** of your choice from this series. Please state below the establishment name, location and your reasons for recommending it.

_____
_____
_____
_____
_____

Please send me **AA Guide** _____

About this guide...

Which title did you buy?

AA _____

Where did you buy it? _____

When? m m / y y

Why did you choose this guide? _____
_____
_____
_____
_____

Did this guide meet your expectations?

Exceeded ☐   Met all ☐   Met most ☐   Fell below ☐

Were there any aspects of this guide that you particularly liked? _____
_____
_____
_____

continued on next page...

Is there anything we could have done better? _____

_____

_____

_____

About you...
Name (Mr/Mrs/Ms) _____

Address _____

_____

_____ Postcode _____

Daytime tel nos _____

Email _____

Please only give us your mobile phone number or email if you wish to hear from us about other products and services from the AA and partners by text or mms, or email.

Which age group are you in?
Under 25 ☐   25–34 ☐   35–44 ☐   45–54 ☐   55–64 ☐   65+ ☐

How many trips do you make a year?
Less than one ☐   One ☐   Two ☐   Three or more ☐

Are you an AA member? Yes ☐   No ☐

About your trip...
When did you book? mm / yy When did you travel? mm / yy

How long did you stay? _____

Was it for business or leisure? _____

Did you buy any other travel guides for your trip? _____

If yes, which ones? _____

_____

_____

Thank you for taking the time to complete this questionnaire. Please send it to us as soon as possible, and remember, you do not need a stamp (unless posted outside the UK).

AA Travel Insurance call 0800 072 4168 or visit www.theAA.com

---